BOOK NEWS

JUL.
Division
1 WEST 3
T

D0757806

Selected Reviews on

ROCKY: The Story of a Champion
by Bill Libby

".... Bill Libby evokes the power, vigor and tenacity of Rocky Marciano, the only heavyweight champion thus far to retire from the ring undefeated. Libby ranges from Marciano's early life in Brockton, Mass., through his rise to the championship, and finally to the fatal plane crash in 1969. The topic is boxing so this is not a gentle book, but there is a sense of compassion and understanding among the famous boxers of Marciano's era."   *School Library Journal*

"The story of Rocky Marchegiano is one which many immigrant boys wished were theirs. He grew up poor, with no liking for education, and by the time he was 30 he was heavyweight champion, a worldwide celebrity with money. Whatever his image in the ring, outside he was soft and gentle, wanting what everyone wanted out of a career, a good time, a nice family and financial security; he thought boxing was the way for him. To Mr. Libby's credit, he makes this portrait credible. He also mentions every pro fight of Marciano's undefeated career, the more important rightly receiving more space; in fact the Louis fight is discussed twice because of the turning point it was for Marciano. There is much emotion expressed in the book and it is hard not to come away feeling sad that such a simple man had to die in the way and at the age that this champ did."   *Kirkus Reviews*

ROCKY
The Story of a Champion

Born: September 1, 1923
Died: August 31, 1969

Books by Bill Libby

THE DICK BASS STORY
ROOKIE GOALIE: GERRY DESJARDINS
ROCKY: THE STORY OF A CHAMPION

ROCKY

The Story of a Champion

by
BILL LIBBY
photographs

Julian Messner Ⓜ   New York

For Joan and Bob Combs, my sister
and brother-in-law, but also my friends.

Contents

Former heavyweight champion Joe Louis crumples through the ropes in eighth round giving the title to Rocky Marciano. *Wide World Photo*

1

A Couple of Champions

A couple of Champions

"He looked like the biggest man I ever saw," Rocky Marciano once said, recalling that October evening in 1951 when he stood across the ring from Joe Louis in the old Madison Square Garden in New York. And "the Brown Bomber" *was* big, even more so in the minds of men than in physical size. He was then the former heavyweight champion of the world, who had held the crown longer and defended it more often than any other man in history. He had been acclaimed an immortal in his own time. But now time was running out on him.

Joe Louis had fought professionally 71 times in 18 years. He was 37 years old, which is old for a fighter, and had been retired for two years, which is a long time for an old fighter to be away from competition. He was in the thirteenth month of his comeback. Rocky Marciano was 28 years old and had fought as a pro only 37 times in five years. He had been fighting regularly, but he had never fought a "big" fight before. He was undefeated, but he had never fought a Joe Louis before.

More than 17,000 persons were crammed into the great old arena. Newsmen were ready at ringside to report the results to millions of sports fans around the world. In the infancy of television, TV cameras were prepared to beam the action into homes across the country. But, outside of Marciano's hometown, few wanted to see this New England cobbler's son topple the old king, who had won public affection with his explosive triumphs and simple, modest personality. Marciano, too, was a simple, modest person, capable of explosive triumphs, but he had yet to earn his place in the boxing world.

Marciano seemed an earnest but clumsy competitor, and few could imagine him beating the great Louis. Marciano could hit hard, but who could punch with Louis? Marciano could attack aggressively, but who could overwhelm the polished, poised Louis? Louis was three inches taller and thirty-five pounds heavier than his squat foe. Louis had a much greater reach. He had much greater experience. He also was nine years older, but no one wanted to think of that then. Even Marciano felt he should not and could not count on that. He admitted later to intense nervousness, which made him sweat and feel sick to his stomach.

"Did you have any fear when you fought?" he once was asked.

"No," he said, "only a fear of shame if I couldn't come home a winner."

"What was the closest you ever came to fear?"

"Facing Joe Louis, who seemed bigger than life. He had been so great, I couldn't imagine myself fighting him and beating him."

"But he was too old."

"I didn't know that until later," Marciano said.

The house lights were turned down until only a single, harsh glare spotlighted the rivals in the ring. The bell rang and the ex-champ and the contender moved at one another; and that great, special tension rose up in all who watched, that frightening feeling that comes when men meet with gloved fists in a modern version of primeval combat. And as they fought, the crowd noise rose and fell with the ebb and flow of battle until there was bedlam in the building, for this turned out to be one of the most dramatic bouts, one of the pivotal moments, in boxing history.

For seven rounds, Louis held Rocky away, left-jabbing him powerfully, counterpunching him cleverly. Most of the time, Louis punched faster and landed first. When Marciano did land, Louis lashed back strongly. Marciano landed some heavy punches on Louis, but he missed more punches than he landed. Louis exploited Marciano's awkwardness. Joe's reflexes had slowed and he could not connect with a knockout blow even when the opening presented itself, but he kept Rocky off balance and at bay and the crowd roared for the valiant, glamorous old gladiator.

Still, Marciano kept coming. It was his way. He looked foolish sometimes. He missed a punch and floundered almost off his feet, but he simply collected himself and resumed coming out of his crouch, hurling long punches upward, hurting Louis whenever he hit him, seemingly beyond being hurt no matter how often he himself was hit. Marciano kept moving forward on those thick legs of his, punching tirelessly. Old Joe's legs began to get heavy. His arms began to get heavy. His breathing was labored. His senses became misted with weariness and pain. He had to force himself to fight on as the crowd roared for him and pleaded with him.

Near the end of the seventh round, Marciano caught the slowing veteran with a barrage of looping left hooks and short right crosses that seemed to stagger Joe and brought the fans to their feet screaming; but Louis bravely fought back, somehow summoning the strength for one more counterassault, landing a left-hand punch to the head that seemed to stun the Rock for a second and thrilled the crowd. Still, when the eighth round began, it was as it had been before, Marciano coming on and Louis fading.

Rocky tried to force Joe into the ropes. Louis drove both hands into Marciano's midsection in an effort to keep him away. He could not. Pressed against the ropes, Louis began to throw a right-hand punch. As he did, Marciano hooked with his left and caught Joe squarely on the chin. It was a devastating punch and dropped the Brown Bomber as though he had been hit with a hammer, and raised his fans as though they had been prodded by electricity.

With the people yelling at him to rise, Joe did, as though from memory, but his mind was clouded and his legs were shaky and his arms hung limp. Marciano moved at him, swinging wildly, missing punches. Then he hit Louis with another left hook squarely on Joe's chin. Louis stood stunned now, knocked out on his feet, his hands dangling at his sides. Marciano threw his right hand, which he called his "Susie-Q," and it glanced off Joe's jaw and struck his neck, and Louis sprawled through the ropes and lay half in and half out of the ring.

Everyone knew it was all over then. The referee did not even have to count. Another great champion, Sugar Ray Robinson, leaped from his seat and ran to the ring, hoisted himself up on the apron of the ring and lifted the Bomber's head off the canvas and cried as he cradled his friend in his arms. A hush fell over the crowd. It was eerie, such silence at this moment of dramatic conclusion. But a king was dead.

"I started to jump for joy," Rocky recalled later, "and then I looked at Louis. I saw him lying there—a great fighter finished—and I remembered his greatness. I just couldn't help feeling sorry for him. I just stood there feeling sort of sad in this moment of joy, and suddenly I knew someday it could be me. And I didn't ever want it to be me, not that way. I thought I would be champion someday, as Joe had been, and I never wanted to lose, not ever. And if I retired, I never wanted to come back, as Joe did, to go too far, to get beaten, to end up lying in the ring with some young guy standing over me and the crowd out there somewhere roaring in the night."

And the crowd had begun to roar. The king was dead now, after all, and a new king was being born. The moments of mourning, the seconds of silent respect, had swiftly come to an end, and suddenly everyone was yelling for this new fellow, this new hero they could idolize. They slapped him on the back and reached out to shake his hand as police escorted Marciano through the mob of well-wishers back to his dressing room, along with his trainer and his manager. While the reporters waited impatiently outside, pounding on the door, Marciano sat, sweaty and sore and weary, and wept. And before he would speak to the writers, he composed a message of admiration and sympathy to be carried to the man he had just beaten into submission.

It is a cruel sport, boxing—primitive and almost senseless. It will probably never again be as popular as it was when Jack Dempsey and Joe Louis and Rocky Marciano reigned over it. But if any moment in the life of any man symbolizes boxing at its best and at its worst, it was the instant when Rocky Marciano smashed down his desperate predecessor. Louis' life went downhill from that moment. Rocky's would yet rise awhile, before turning downward. Behind him lay an erratic and difficult rise to this point in his history. Ahead of him lay Jersey Joe Walcott, a shot at the title and a date with destiny.

Few men were so well suited for a boxing career as

Marciano, with his rugged body and large, heavy hands and incredible determination. And few so poorly prepared for it as this man with his quiet, gentle manner and his distaste for hurting anyone. "It's all I got to do that I can do," he shrugged simply. This he found out along the way.

Rocky in 1940, when he was a member of the Whit-
man Junior High School baseball team. *United
Press Photo*

2

Rocco Marchegiano

"I always knew he'd be a champion someday," Rocky Marciano's father said after his son had won the heavyweight title. "I didn't know champion of what—football, baseball, boxing—but I knew he'd be a champion of something."

Perrino Marchegiano (pronounced "Mark-a-John-o") came from Chieti, a tiny fishing village near the Adriatic, in Italy, to Brockton, Massachusetts, a small industrial town in New England. Brockton's main business was shoemaking, and Marchegiano, a shoemaker in the old country, continued his trade in the New World.

However, he fought for the United States in World War I. With the Army's Second Division in the Argonne Forest in France in 1917, he was severely gassed, and returned to America underweight and sickly. While he recovered, he never regained his full strength. From then on, he hammered out a hard, meager living in the shoe factory. He was a willing worker, but short and thin and sickly.

Luigi Picciutto, a six-foot-one, 220-pound blacksmith, came

17

to the United States from San Bartolomeo, near Naples, in 1918, and brought his family over the following year, settling them in Brockton. One of his daughters, Pasqualena, married Perrino Marchegiano.

In 1922, she lost her first child in birth. "If God want me to have baby, I have baby," she said later. The following year, at 1:00 A.M., September 1, Dr. Josephat Phaneuf delivered her a 13-pound 2-ounce son, who was named Rocco Francis.

She asked the doctor, "How much this cost?"

He said, "Forty dollars."

She said, "Well, doctor, I give you cash."

"Well, then, thirty-five dollars," he said.

This was during the Depression. The Marchegianos lived on Warren Street, but when Rocco was one year old they moved to 80 Brook Street, into his maternal grandfather's white-frame, two-story house, where Rocco was reared. When Rocco was two, he contracted pneumonia. He was critically ill for a while, and the members of the family took turns tending him. He passed the crisis, rallied, survived and regained his strength and health.

A husky, hearty woman, Lena Marchegiano had six children in seventeen years. Following Rocco in order came Alice, Connie, Elizabeth, Louis and Peter, three sons and three daughters. "I keep my house clean. I keep my children clean. I tell my children, now try your best in the school," she said once when asked her philosophy of caring for her family.

Rocco once said, "I get my strength from my mother and my restraint from my father."

It was not an easy life for the Marchegianos. They lived in the two-bedroom upper section of the house. The parents slept in one bedroom, often with the latest baby. The daughters slept in the other bedroom. Rocco slept in the living room, on a mattress laid on the floor. When Louis was growing up, he slept downstairs in his grandfather's part of the house.

There was no central heating, no running hot water, no bathtub. The grandfather kept two coal stoves burning downstairs during the winter, and the Marchegianos kept their doors open at the head of the stairs so some heat could rise to them. Mrs. Marchegiano always had water heating on the stove. The family bathed in a tin washtub in the kitchen. The boys got a bath one Saturday night, the girls the next.

The Marchegianos were patriotic Italian-Americans devoted to their new country, but they never totally severed all ties to the old country. They had a strong nationalistic feeling and always felt closest to others who came from Italy, especially those not so long removed from its shores. Their menus were Italian. They spoke a lot of Italian. Their closest friends tended to be Italian, and they belonged to neighborhood Italian-American clubs, where the old men played bocci. But they were closest to family.

They were Catholic and religious. They attend church regularly and usually worshipped in a family group. There were religious pictures, statues and symbols in their home. When Rocco recovered from pneumonia, Lena Marchegiano donated what little jewelry she had to the church in gratitude for having had her prayers seemingly answered.

They were plain, hard-working people who did not have much, but practiced the old-fashioned virtues of family life, honesty, thrift and the pursuit of simple pleasures. Among these pleasures was wine, which Rocco's grandfather made in the cellar. This was Prohibition time, but Italians did not like to be denied the fruit of the grape. They would not break the law in other ways, but bent this law a bit. They did not sell their bootleg wine, but made it and drank it.

At the risk of contracting pneumonia again, Rocco always slept alongside a window which he kept wide open except in the coldest weather. He loved the fresh air. He disliked school, where he felt confined and cramped. He did not come from a bookish, scholarly family and he was not good at his studies. Later, like so many others, he regretted this early disinterest in school.

At seven, he began to make home deliveries of the local newspaper. His mother sent his five-year-old sister to walk with him along his route for "protection," feeling strangers would be less likely to approach two children than one child. Rocco's pals teased him about this and he hated it.

He admired toughness and strength. He wanted muscles and a powerful body. He first built muscles helping his grandfather haul crates of grapes to the cellar and then helping him mix the thick fluid into wine, though he, himself, never developed a taste for it, or any hard drink. He used to chin himself fifteen times every morning and fifteen times every evening on the limb of a tree in his backyard. "I wanted to be the strongest guy around," he said. He did not grow tall, but he did grow thick and powerful.

He and his next-door neighbor and best buddy, Allie

Colombo, haunted the James J. Edgar Playground between Brook Street, where he lived at the time, and Dover Street, where his parents later lived. They played baseball and football, mainly, and Rocco was good at both. He was a hard hitter even then.

When Rocco was born, among the cards of congratulations his parents received was one that had tiny toy boxing gloves attached and an inscription, "Hail to the Champ." It was just a joke, which had no special meaning at the time, but it proved to be curiously prophetic. And, strangely, Rocco's dad always saved the card.

Rocco's dad had no time or energy to help his son in sports, but his uncle, John Picciutto, did. "My pop was always tired after work and never took me anyplace. I went everywhere with Uncle Johnny," Rocky said. It was John who introduced Rocco to boxing.

In June of 1933, Primo Carnera stopped Jack Sharkey in six rounds to win the world heavyweight boxing championship. Later, the six-foot-six, 260-pound giant's record became suspect, but at the time he was a great hero among his fellow Italians. That year he came to referee a bout in Brockton at the old Centre Street Arena, and Uncle John took nine-year-old Rocco to see him. "On the way out, Carnera walked right by me and I reached out and touched him," Rocky recalled later with wistful wonder. "I ran home and told my dad, 'I saw Carnera and I touched him, I really did.' And dad asked me how big he was. And I said, 'He was bigger than this ceiling.'"

Later, Rocco told his father, "Someday when I grow up, I'll be boxing champion and make one hundred thousand dollars and take care of you and Ma and the kids." His uncle John hung a heavy bag in the basement and had Rocco punch it, teaching him "the noble art of self-defense." He tried to get him to use his left hand as well as his right hand, not only in boxing but in baseball and other sports. He admired men who could use both hands with equal dexterity. He, himself, had a crippled left arm from a boyhood accident, when he fell down a flight of stairs.

Uncle John managed Rocco in his first real "bout." He put him in a midget boxing free-for-all. Four youngsters entered a ring blindfolded and fought until only one was standing. Rocco was not the winner of this one, but as time passed he grew stronger and more efficient with his fists. Allie's uncle set up a ring in his backyard, and Allie promoted a fight between Rocco and Jimmy DiStasi. "We used such great big gloves, we couldn't hurt each other," Rocky laughed. "He used to go around after I became champ saying he went ten with Rocky Marciano."

Julie Durham did not go ten. He was a tough neighborhood kid who used to be mascot for the town baseball team. Another kid, Izzy Gold, got his hands on a foul ball one time and Julie charged up to him, saying, "Gimme that ball or I'll break your head."

Rocky remembered stepping in and suggesting, "Why don't you pick on a guy your size?"

"You want to fight?" Julie challenged.

"Sure, I'll fight you," Rocco said.

Julie threw a punch and knocked Rocco down. Rocco got up and threw a punch and knocked Julie down, and he did not get up. "Now I was a neighborhood big shot," Rocky recalled. "I was still only about twelve."

For a while, others challenged him, but his reputation got so big, he soon was avoided. He had found he did not like to fight, anyway. His dad said, "When he was only thirteen, he told me he was afraid to hit anybody for fear of hurting him bad." His mom remembers, "Rocco was the best-natured child you ever see. I used to spank him for fighting. He never liked it, to hurt anyone. And I no like him to hurt anyone, or maybe be hurt himself."

Uncle John persisted, but Rocco's budding boxing career ended for a while when Uncle John took him to Pat Mc-Gowan's Knights of Columbus gym to try out against a local pro, who gave the willing, strong but inexperienced and untrained amateur a bad beating. "He almost made me never want to box again," Rocky laughingly recalled later.

Rocco was more interested in becoming a professional football or baseball player at the time. He was a 150-pound center on coach Marion Roberts' Brockton High School varsity eleven as a fifteen-year-old sophomore and a good, promising performer, who might have grown into a college career had he continued with it. However, he did not like school and got his excuse to leave from his uncle, who one day said, "Rocco, I think you should go to work. I know where you can make four dollars a day. Your folks can use the money. You know your father isn't too well."

At the dinner table, Rocco told his family he was going to quit school to go to work. "Uncle John can get me a good job," he said.

His mother was upset. "No, no," she protested, "you got to finish school."

But Rocco said, "Look, I'm not a good student. I don't like school. I can make twenty dollars a week and play so much baseball that I can be in the big leagues in a few years."

Uncle John came to the house and he and Mrs. Marchegiano argued. Mr. Marchegiano stayed out of it. In the end, Rocky had his way. He quit school and went to work. He told his mother, "I promise you I'll go to night school and maybe even graduate." Rocky did not keep his promise.

He went to work on a coal truck for fifty cents an hour, eight hours a day, five days a week. He helped deliver heavy buckets of coal. Later, he helped deliver beer. He worked as a candy mixer in a factory. He worked in the shoe factory. He worked as a dishwasher. He worked as a short-order cook. He worked for a landscape gardener. He worked for the city, clearing brush for a blimp hangar in South Weymouth. Then he joined a construction gang, building the Myles Standish Embarkation Station in Taunton. He made $1.25 an hour. This was wartime now, World War II, and Rocky at nineteen was making a fast fifty bucks a week, knocking around from job to job.

When he wasn't working, he was playing baseball, for American Legion teams, for the Sons of Italy, for the Italian-Americans, for the St. Patrick's CYO, for the Ward Two Social Club, for the Brockton Pros, who were semipros. "I used to play seven, eight games a week. I was out for a good time when I was off the job," Rocky boasted. And his idea of a good time at that time was playing some ball and then sitting around sweaty, sipping soft drinks and bulling with the boys.

He had dates, whom he took to dances and movies, but he was not a fast man with the ladies or a slick lad on the dance floor, nor did he have much money. His face was already mashed in with a busted nose, suffered not in boxing, but playing football, when he was stepped on by a teammate in a semipro game. He was a simple, shy guy, who loved baseball. But no big-league scouts were beating down the doors of his house to sign him. So he worked at hard labor.

"I liked the pick-and-shovel work a lot better than being in the factory. I couldn't stand being cooped up all day. I couldn't stand the smell of the shoe leather or the candy. I had to be out in the air," he said. He recalled how as a boy he carried lunch to his pop in the shoe factory and how the old man shook his head and said, "Be somebody, Rocco. Don't never work in a factory." But Rocky had few alternatives. He said, "I saw what the factory had done to my father and I didn't want it to happen to me, but there didn't seem to be much for me."

Then, in March of 1943, at nineteen, he was drafted into the Army. He was processed through the same base he had helped build. He was given recruit training and assigned to the 150th Combat Engineers, moved around New England from Camp Standish to Camp Pickett to Fort Devins. He later laughed, "They took one look at me and knew what I was good for. I was a ditch-digger in uniform. Boy, did we sweat." However, he was used to that and he didn't mind it.

He got three square meals a day, a roof over his head, a warm bed, a small check and an allotment sent home to his family every month.

His outfit then was shipped overseas to England, where it was to help prepare for the Allies' projected invasion of German-held France. On the ship, the *Mauretania*, jammed with soldiers, who killed time gambling, tight-fisted Marchegiano borrowed a quarter from a buddy to try his luck at a blackjack game. He built his twenty-five cents into eight dollars and tried a poker game. He built his eight dollars into fifty dollars and tried shooting dice. He walked away with $1,200, more money than he had made in five months of working.

Perhaps it gave him a taste for "quick, easy money." If he could have mailed it home right then, he probably would have done so. Instead, when the ship reached England, his buddies, who had not been paid for a long time and had gambled away their pocket money, begged him for loans to finance liberties. Good-natured, wanting to be liked, Rocky passed most of the money out. He got very little of it back. "When I repaid the quarter I borrowed, I gave the guy a good piece of my winnings. He wound up with more money than me in the end," Rocky later recalled. "Maybe it was all worthwhile. It taught me a good lesson. I was never too free with my money after that."

Stationed in Wales, Rocky got a reputation of being a tough guy. He said, "I wasn't boxing then, but I was pretty rough in baseball and football games and I also had some sessions with three wrestlers, who tried to pin me and couldn't." Also, he looked the part.

There was a tough Texan on the base who was bullying some of the guys, and Rocco's buddies wanted him to take care of the fellow. "He had been making things unpleasant for a lot of the boys and they kept asking me to take him on and give him a lesson. Finally, I agreed to fight this guy. It was on a Saturday afternoon. The boys formed a circle and we put on the gloves. I stopped him in two rounds. He quit while he was on the ground. He stopped bothering the fellows."

He had another fight, at a pub in England. A "local lad," a very large "local lad," who clearly didn't like "Yanks" and who had a few too many drinks in him, began to ridicule Rocco's group and the Coke-drinking Marchegiano. One of Rocco's buddies suggested he was the fighter and he should take on this wise guy. The wise guy thought this was very funny and challenged Rocco, calling him a few imaginative names. "He was the biggest fellow I ever saw," Rocky recalled. "And it turned out he could box some. I threw a wild punch, hit him just right and knocked him out. I was very lucky." When the "local lad" was revived, he introduced himself as an Australian regimental boxing champion, admired Rocky's punch, apologized for taunting him and shook hands with him.

The invasion came and Rocky's outfit ferried supplies back and forth across the English Channel to Normandy until no longer needed. When Germany surrendered, Rocky's outfit was returned to the United States and assigned to Fort Lewis, Washington. Here there was a recreational boxing program and those of Rocky's group who had seen him fight in the streets or saloons encouraged him to try his luck.

To get out of extra duty, Rocco did so. And, not surprisingly as it turned out, he did well.

He knew little about serious fighting, but then neither did most of his foes. He was strong and could take punishment and hit hard. He was given leave to enter the National AAU tournament in Portland, Oregon. He broke a knuckle' on a finger on his left hand winning the semifinal, went on without telling anyone of his injury and lost a decision in the final to Joe DeAngelis, although he knocked DeAngelis down at the final bell. DeAngelis later tried for a boxing career, but retired with heart trouble.

An Army doctor repaired Rocky's finger with a delicate operation and two months of treatment. Rocky later gratefully sought to reward this fellow, a Japanese-American who had saved his career, but he had forgotten his name and never was able to locate him. However, this was not the last hand injury Rocky suffered. His hands used to stiffen and swell up after most of his fights. He was lucky in being able to score many quick knockouts. He seldom had to subject his hands to excessive punishment and never suffered a crippling injury. He had big, heavy hands and a powerful grip which he strengthened by squeezing a hard rubber ball constantly, but they never were strong hands.

Transferred back to a base in Massachusetts, he was reunited with old buddy Allie Colombo, a sergeant in the Air Force, assigned to nearby Westover Field. Colombo, hearing of Rocco's amateur boxing success, encouraged him to turn pro. He spoke to a former fighter, Dick O'Connor, who was a customs inspector at the camp. O'Connor called up Oriele Renault, who was putting on fights in Holyoke.

Rocco was offered a four-round preliminary bout. Rocco wasn't sure he was ready, but he agreed, only after it was suggested he try under an assumed name to protect his amateur standing. He used the name "Rocky Mack." The Mack did not stick, but the Rocky did.

Rocky was promised fifty dollars. He fought one Lee Epperson. This was on the night of St. Patrick's Day, March 17, 1947. Rocky took a beating until he connected with a wild roundhouse in the third, and Epperson went down for the ten count. "I didn't like it," Rocco said. "It was a tough fight and seemed a tough way to make a buck." He liked it even less when he was handed fifteen dollars. He and Allie raised cain until the promoter came across with more money. Rocky walked away dissatisfied with the sport.

Discharged in midyear, he returned to Brockton and found a job working on a construction gang for ninety cents an hour. He had to pay a union man fifty dollars to get the job, paying it out over a period of several weeks. When he had paid up, he was fired. He bounced to a job that brought him bigger money—a dollar an hour—laying gas mains for the Brockton Gas Company. Civilian life seemed less than sweet to him. He was twenty-three years old and he was no one, getting nowhere.

He was still playing baseball, semipro ball, and hoping he could make something of himself in the sport, though that hope seemed slim by then. He was catching and hitting well, but he'd gotten a sore arm pitching in a game in Swansea and he was not throwing well. Ralph Wheeler, a Boston schoolboy sportswriter, scouting for the Chicago Cubs on the side, was impressed with the strong Ward Two club of Brockton and arranged for a southern tryout for several of the players, including Allie Colombo's brother, Ritchie, and cousin, Gene Sylvester. Gene had pitched to Rocky often, was his pal and touted him until he was included in the group.

They went to Fayetteville, North Carolina, where they joined the Cubs' minor-league team. Rocky hit well, but he simply could not make a strong, snap throw from behind the plate to second base and he did not seem agile enough to fit in anywhere else, so he was rejected. "All my friends knew I'd gone and had sent me off with good wishes and high hopes and I'd failed. I was ashamed and hated to go home," Rocky later admitted. Another Brockton recruit, Red Gormley, had arranged another tryout, with the Goldsboro Bugs in Wilson, North Carolina. Rocky went with him and played a few games but the results were the same. "The manager finally told me I'd better go home," Rocky sighed. Now, he had no alternative.

Red flunked out, too. He drove Rocky home in an old car. Both boys were very depressed. During the long ride back, Rocky reached a decision. Baseball had beaten him. He didn't want to go back to a pick and shovel. Somehow he wanted to make a decent living for himself. He didn't really like boxing, but he seemed rugged enough to have a chance, and he determined to give it an all-out effort. It was his last hope, his only real hope for something special.

Red later recalled Rocco saying, "The heck with it. I'm through with baseball. I'm gonna get some fights and you're gonna handle me. I can make a lot of money. You can manage me and make a lot of money, too." Red smiled and shrugged it off. It was just talk, he knew. They were both disappointed. He knew neither of them was going to make a lot of money. He was no fight manager. He became a mailman. Years later, he sighed and said, "There I was sitting next to half the money in the world and I didn't know it." His chance came and went. But Rocco Marchegiano's chance lay just ahead of him, waiting for him, and he had turned a corner and was headed for it now.

Heavyweight champion Jersey Joe Walcott hammers at Rocky Marciano as the challenger bends over in third round of the title fight. Rocky won the crown with a knockout victory in the thirteenth round. *Wide World Photo*

3

Allie, Al and Charlie

Returning home from his aborted baseball career, Rocco Marchegiano announced to his parents that he was going to become a boxer. His father said, "Why not? You're strong enough. Try." His mother said, "If it's what you want. Be careful."

Allie Colombo volunteered to help him and made contact with Generoso Caggiano, a bus mechanic who fancied himself a fight manager and promoted amateur cards at Hibernian Hall. Although he already had fought once professionally under the name of "Rocky Mack," Rocco resumed as an "amateur" for thirty dollars a fight.

Although he knew nothing about the science of boxing and was extremely awkward, few of his foes knew more or had more polish. Rocco was stronger, more willing to absorb punishment and a heavier hitter than most of the men he faced, and he won consistently until he went to New York to fight at Ridgewood Grove in Brooklyn in the Eastern Golden Gloves Tournament. Here, on March 1, 1948, he was outpointed by Coley Wallace. They fought the three two-minute rounds, but Rocky couldn't get through to the more accomplished Wallace. Coley later had some success as a pro but achieved his greatest fame by portraying Joe Louis in a movie about the Brown Bomber's career.

Allie and Rocco and those around him felt he had some chance to make it as a professional, but needed professional help. Allie gave up his job in order to devote full time to helping his friend, living off his savings and hoping, of course, to cash in eventually.

A number of persons had a chance to sign Rocco then, but did not take advantage of it. Al Silverman, a Boston promoter and manager, watched Rocco throughout much of his amateur career, but did not think enough of his future to tie him up. Peter Fuller, the son of a former governor of Massachusetts and a former amateur fighter who had ambitions of managing a heavyweight champion, talked of paying Rocco $1,000 for his signature, which the poor, hungry Marchegiano camp would have grabbed, but Fuller never got around to it.

Eddie Boland, a New England boxing man, suggested to Allie that what Rocco really needed was a New York fight manager. This was the hub of world boxing at that time and a New York manager with good connections could get a boy a good trainer and get him bouts. He recommended Al Weill. Allie wrote Al in part, "We are interested mainly in a manager in New York who has the contacts to take care of a very promising heavyweight property. Believe me, he has tremendous possibilities."

Weill, who knew Marchegiano's name from his Golden Gloves loss to Wallace, turned the letter over to his trainer,

Charlie Goldman, who sent Colombo a note telling him to bring his boy in on a certain date for a tryout. Broke and not wanting to borrow the money for fare, Allie and Rocco missed the appointment waiting for a free ride into New York with a friend who drove a fruit and vegetable truck into the big city several times a week.

They arrived a day late at Weill's office in the 1500 block on Broadway. Al Weill was a short, fat man, nicknamed "the Vest" because he got all the gravy. He had a foghorn voice, always had a cigar in his mouth, wore thick eyeglasses and was given to sporting a yachting cap.

His reputation was not the best because he was friendly with Frankie Carbo, a hoodlum who had interests in boxing and reportedly had a piece of Weill's action. It was an unfortunate fact that many mobsters had boxing interests, and without his connections in this area, Weill probably would not have been able to operate effectively. And he had operated effectively, guiding featherweight Joey Archibald, lightweight Lou Ambers and welterweight Marty Servo to the world titles in their division before hooking up with Marchegiano. Apparently, Rocco never dealt with Carbo, met him only once or twice to shake his hand and never was exposed to the seamy side of the sport.

Weill's trainer was Charlie Goldman, a great bantamweight in the early 1900's, a tiny five-footer, who was a giant strategist, a fellow who, like his boss, did not speak precise English, but communicated well with fighters. He was with Weill in his office when Allie Colombo brought Rocco Marchegiano in that afternoon in May of 1948, right off a fruit and vegetable truck. They were poor boys, dressed poorly. "They looked as if they had come to sweep the place up," Goldman recalled later.

"I was so scared, I couldn't speak," Rocky said.

"Who told you you could fight?" Weill asked Rocco in his direct, brusque way.

"He won all the fights he's been in," said Colombo, answering for the nervous Rocco, ignoring, among others, the Wallace bout.

Understanding such exaggeration, Weill let it pass. "How many amateur fights you had?" he asked.

"About twelve," Colombo said.

"Can you punch?" Weill asked.

"Oh, ho," Colombo snorted, as if it was the most ridiculous question ever asked.

"With the right hand?"

"With both," Colombo said.

Fight managers frequently say "we." They send their tigers out to slaughter lambs as if they were extensions of themselves. The managers do not take the punishment, but they consider themselves and their fighters single entities: "We beat this guy from here to there, but it was his hometown so they give him the decision." In some cases, they take the credit and pass on the blame. "We won big," or "He wasn't paying attention to me and so he blew it."

However, none of this minimizes the importance of a manager to a fighter. Boxers do not have schedules like baseball or football teams. Each match must be arranged. If a fighter is to do well it must be the right match for his ability and at terms equal to his importance. Managers must maneuver with other managers and promoters for the best bouts. They take their cut and often earn it, frequently bankrolling a beginner who could not get started any other way until he began to return a profit. And most fighters never make it big.

Weill was perfectly willing to let Colombo speak for Marchegiano, but he was also prepared to disregard him in the future. Weill was considering taking on a fighter, and if he took him on, he would be the manager, not this buddy of the fighter's.

"How much does he weigh?" he asked.

"One-ninety," Colombo said, identifying himself as an outsider. A boxing man simply would have said "ninety," and the one hundred would have been assumed.

"How old is he?" Weill asked.

"Twenty-three," Colombo admitted reluctantly.

Weill frowned. That was old for a fellow to begin a boxing career. Fighters usually begin as teen-agers and have won titles at twenty and twenty-one.

Weill turned to Goldman. "Let's take him over to the gym and see what he looks like."

Rocco, sitting scared like a puppet, still had not said a word.

"Let's go," Goldman said.

They went to the Catholic Youth Organization gym on 17th Street, where Goldman trained Weill's fighters and where other boxers worked out. Stillman's Gym was the big boxing gym in New York, and Bobby Gleason's Gym in the Bronx hosted its share of top men, but Weill and others worked out of the CYO spot.

They got Rocco into some equipment and warmed him up. First Goldman put him to punching the light and heavy bags. "He didn't even know how to punch the bags, but I saw he had strong arms," Charlie recalled later. Then they put him in the ring to spar with a journeyman pro, Wade Chancey. Goldman told Chancey to "work this kid over and see if he's got anything."

Chancey did. He knew enough about boxing to make the kid look bad. He avoided Rocco's wild punches and slipped inside his crude defenses to punish him. They were wearing headgear and using heavy gloves, but still Rocco took a bad beating. At one point he simply raised both hands over his head to absorb the rain of blows that were being sent his way. Then, angrily, he lashed out with a wild right hand which landed heavily on Chancey's head, startling and stunning him. He stood still, blinking, and Goldman hollered, "Time," and jumped into the ring to stop it.

Years later, Goldman recalled his feelings at this time: "If he did anything right, I didn't see it," he said, "and I told him that. He was a real green clumsy kid. He was short and didn't have any kind of reach. And he was twenty-three years old going on twenty-four, which was awful old to just start teaching someone this business. But he was a quiet kid and seemed sincere. I could see he wanted to be a fighter and was willing to work. He didn't seem afraid in the ring. I knew he was hungry. I figured he had an all-around athletic background, which might help. I could see he had strong arms and could punch, which is the big thing. I figured maybe he had a chance to do something, not as a champion, mind you, but just as a good pro maybe."

Weill didn't like what he saw, except that he liked the kid's punch. He went around asking other managers what they thought of him, and they told him they didn't like what they saw, except they liked the kid's punch. At least one said, "Are you kidding, Al? He's got no chance. Forget it."

Weill went to Goldman and said, "He's got no chance."

Goldman said, "Maybe he's not too bad."

Weill said, "Ah, he's got two left feet. I seen it."

Goldman said, "Let him stick around a couple of days until I look at him."

Weill shrugged. He said it was all right as long as it didn't cost too much. He fished a twenty-dollar bill out of his pocket and handed it over. Goldman put Rocco and Colombo up at a nearby YMCA. They ate dinner in the cafeteria, talking hopefully about their chances. "He didn't sign me," Rocco said. "He didn't turn you away," Colombo pointed out.

Goldman worked with Rocco in the gym. Two days later, he told Weill, "That Marchegiano don't look bad at all. He can hit, but he needs a lot of work."

Weill said, "You mean that guy's still here? We don't pay him no expenses, understand. I got enough broken-down fighters. This guy ain't even broken down yet. He ain't got enough talent to be broken down."

Goldman said the kid was real green and awkward, of course, and built pretty short—and no kid, really. But he was strong and willing and he could hit, and maybe they ought to sign him just to protect themselves for a little while and see if they could maybe do a little something with him.

Weill thought about it. He was tempted to just let it go. Who needed another headache? Still, Charlie seemed to think the guy had a chance. And heavyweights are the most precious commodity in boxing, if not in all of sports. A good heavyweight could make money. A great one could make a lot of money. Most fighters were black or Puerto Rican or Mexican, poor kids who turned to the ring in desperation. A good white heavyweight could be a gate attraction. Chances are this kid wouldn't be good, much less great, but it wouldn't cost much to tie him up for a little while, just to see.

Al Weill had the most important decision of his life to make, though he did not know that then. OK, he shrugged. He'd sign him and let Charlie work with him, but he wouldn't pay any expenses he didn't have to pay until the kid showed him something, which he probably never would, and he was a sucker for even thinking so. He told Charlie to have the kid come to his office—the kid, not the other guy with him.

Rocco Marchegiano went into the office and came out a professional fighter. Weill told him he'd have Goldman train him and get him some fights and see if he could do something with him. In New York? Rocco asked. Back home, Weill said. Anytime you can get to town, Charlie will work with you. Back home, you practice what he teaches you. You work hard, see. I got a friend promoting fights out your way. Providence's out your way, isn't it? Rocky said, about thirty miles from Brockton. Fine, Weill said. You train and we'll get you some fights and we'll see what we can do for you. He didn't say he wouldn't be at those fights and neither, most of the time, would Goldman.

He shoved a contract across the desk at Rocco and told him to sign it. It called for Weill to get 50 percent of Rocco's earnings. Rocco looked at it and asked about Colombo: He'd been managing him. He'd been helping him. He was his friend. Could Allie get cut in, maybe for, say, 10 percent? No chance, Weill said. He didn't know anything about what Colombo was to Rocco. That was before, anyway. This was now. Now Al Weill was going to be his manager. If Al Weill was going to manage him, Al Weill was going to manage him. No one else, not even Charlie Goldman, got a cut of the contract. Weill had Goldman on salary. If Rocco wanted to put Colombo on salary, that was his business. If he wanted to slip him something, that was his business. Rocco looked at his lap. Then he signed the contract.

Rocco walked out and went to Colombo. We got us a big-time manager, he told Allie. Where did he fit in? Allie asked. Don't worry, I'll take care of you, Rocky said. You're with me. You have my word. It was good. As long as he fought, Allie Colombo, his buddy who had helped him get his start, was by his side, helping him and getting his cut, but from Rocky, not Weill.

Goldman began to work with Rocco. After a few days, Rocco went back to Brockton. He'd met a girl, Barbara Cousens, at a dance. She was a policeman's daughter, a big blonde, a lovely girl, and he liked her and had begun to go steady with her. He told her he had a big-time manager and was going to become a professional boxer, now. She said if that was what he wanted, it was all right with her. She could even help. A friend of her father's, Russ Murray, had a big house in Raynham Park with a gym in it, which Rocco could use for training.

With Allie's help, Rocco began to train hard, trying to master everything Goldman showed him. Seven days a week, he worked. In the mornings, he did roadwork, running many miles to build up his legs, his breathing, his endurance. In the afternoons, he worked in the gym, building up his speed on the light bag and his punching power on the heavy bag, and sparring with anyone available. Every week or two, he hitched a ride on the fruit and vegetable truck into New York to work out with Goldman.

Charlie recalls, "We had to start from scratch. His stance and stride were way too long, throwing him way off balance. He threw his punches way too long, telegraphing them. He punched with his arms. He didn't get his shoulders or body into his punches. He didn't even know how to hold his hands. He was wide open. He jabbed with his left palm held up. He didn't punch hard with his left. He threw one punch at a time. He stood straight up and was so short and had such short arms he couldn't reach the other guy half the time."

Goldman tied his feet together to shorten his stride. He got him to fight out of a crouch so he'd be harder to hit. He taught him how to hold his hands with his left hand in front of his face to protect his jaw and block punches, and he taught him how to move his right hand in front of his face when he punched with his left hand. He taught him to hook as well as jab with his left, although it was a long time before his left hand was nearly as effective as his right, and he never did learn to jab too strongly. Nor did he ever become stylish, though gradually he mastered the mechanics.

Goldman taught him to throw his punches in combinations of twos and threes, to punch to the body as well as to the head. He draped a towel behind his back and made him hold on to the ends while punching to shorten up his punches and to pivot at the hips to get his weight behind the blows. He worked on speeding up Rocco's hands, but not his feet. "His legs were too heavy and we didn't want to monkey with his style too much for fear we'd spoil his natural power," Charlie said. "He didn't learn fast, but he learned. He listened better than any fighter I ever taught."

Rocco had no money. Once he asked Weill for fifteen dollars and was refused. You got to earn it first, he was told. He and Allie got by somehow. They'd stay at Ma Brown's Rooming House or the "Y" overnight, then ride back to Brockton on the truck. In New York, he was in the shadows, but looking at spotlighted souls, dazzled by the glamour of big names.

He got a reputation as a tremendous puncher. Once Jack Dempsey brought in Joe Weider, a heavyweight from Vienna he was thinking of managing. He asked Goldman if he could put him in the ring with Rocco. He said to Rocco, "Kid, I want you to hit this guy right in the chin because I want to see if he can take a punch." Rocky hit him in the face and split it open and the fellow began to bleed. Dempsey took him to the hospital, then sent him home.

Rocky and Allie spotted Willie Pep, the featherweight champion, leaving the gym with a girl. Willie was dressed beautifully and his girl was a beauty. They followed the couple. Pep stopped by a vendor and bought his girl a flower, pinning it on her shoulder and kissing her on the forehead. Then he turned into a theater with her. "It was beautiful," Rocco said later. "We just wanted to see what life was like for a champion, and we could see he had class," he said. Once, when they had a few bucks, they tried to go into Leone's, the famous Italian restaurant, but were refused because they were not wearing ties. Years later, they got in with or without ties.

Rocco was dedicated. When he swam in the YMCA pool, he threw punches underwater to build up his speed and striking power, for example. He did not suddenly become graceful or quick, but he gradually became very good with what he had. And Weill began to get him fights as promised, with Manny Almeida, who was promoting cards in Providence. Frequently, Rocco walked the thirty miles to Providence to build up his legs and save money. When he got there, he and Colombo were alone, but Almeida and his aides looked after him, on instructions from Weill. He fought seven straight times in Providence over three months.

On July 12, 1948, he began his second pro career with his second pro fight, knocking out Harry Balzerian in one round. He was paid forty dollars. A week later, he knocked out John Edwards in one round. Three weeks later, he knocked out Bobby Quinn in three rounds. After every fight, he went to New York to report to Goldman and work under him. Allie had gotten married, and his father gave him a 1935 car to chauffeur Rocky back and forth, which helped.

Two weeks later, Rocco knocked out Eddie Ross in one

round. He was not being put in with the best fighters
around, but he was just a beginner and some of his foes were
not too bad. For instance, Ross had previously been undefeated in 25 fights, winning 21 of them by knockouts.
After this one, Almeida called Weill excitedly to tell him he
really should come see his new boy work. Weill sent Goldman, who joined Colombo in Rocco's corner. Rocco knocked
out Jimmy Weeks in one. Goldman returned with Rocco,
praising him to Weill. At the end of August, Goldman returned to Providence and saw Rocco flatten Jerry Jackson
in one. This kid's some kind of hitter, he told Weill.

Weill was getting interested now. He was talking to Almeida on the telephone every day and he had about decided
he might have a diamond in the rough. He wanted to polish
him. They agreed he had to change his name. No one could
spell Marchegiano, much less pronounce it. Rocco was already being called Rocky. That was fine. But Marchegiano
had to go. Rocky protested: it was his name. It's like being
an actor, Weill explained. If you're going to be big in the
business, you have to have a name people can handle. Like
Joe Louis. Or Sugar Ray Robinson. Or Willie Pep. What
was Pep's real name—Papaleo? No one used their real name
in boxing. Joe Louis was really Joe Louis Barrow. Sugar
Ray Robinson was Walker Smith. Rocky could be the Brockton . . . Blockbuster. Or the Brockton Strong Man. Like
John L. Sullivan, the Boston Strong Man. But Marchegiano
had to go.

How about "Rocky Mack," which he had used in his first
pro fight? No good, Rocky protested. It didn't sound Italian
enough. He was Italian. He was proud of it. Weill knew it

helped a fighter's publicity sometimes to have him identi-
fied with a national group. He was on the phone with Almeida, who suggested simply dropping the middle part of
his name. Weill wrote Marchegiano down and scratched out
the middle "heg." That left Marciano. That didn't seem too
bad. "March-e-ano," he said. "Mar-si-ano." That's OK. Is
that OK? Rocky shrugged. It was OK, he supposed. If it
had to be, it had to be.

So he was Rocky Marciano. But he never changed it
legally as long as he fought. "My real name is Marchegiano,"
he once said. "It's my father's name and my brother's name.
They're not gonna change it because of me. And I'm not
gonna change it. I wouldn't want them to feel bad."

The next week, Rocky Marciano knocked out Bill Harde-
man in one round. Now Rocky had eight straight knockouts
as a pro, six in the first round, the last four in a row. Weill
liked what he heard. The kid was tough and he hit hard. He
hadn't been tested yet, but he'd been taking everyone out
quick. Weill began to take a real interest, plotting his career
carefully, picking his foes carefully. He wanted to keep him
winning, but progressing, building him up. He wanted to
show him around a little, too.

He set up a match for him with Gil Cardione in Washington, D.C. Rocky scored another first-round KO. In less
than a week he was back in Providence to box Bob Jefferson. Jefferson lasted two rounds. Weill's head was beginning
to whirl. He brought Rocky to New York, put him up at a
boardinghouse and put him through two months of inten-
sive training without any more fights. He didn't want to
take any chances of spoiling what suddenly seemed a good

thing. He wanted Rocky to be ready. Rocky progressed steadily until Weill tossed him back into the pit, in Providence, against Pat Connolly. Rocky flattened him in the first round.

His record was beginning to make an impression on the boxing crowd and on the sportswriters and Weill was beginning to tout him grandly, though he had not yet seen him, himself. He never admitted this. Some said his opposition was suspect, but Weill waved them off, saying he had something good going for him and he wasn't going to throw him to the wolves, ruining him by rushing him.

In mid-December, Joe Louis was booked to box Arturo Godoy in an exhibition in Philadelphia, and Weill booked Marciano for a preliminary bout against Gilley Ferron on the undercard and he went, himself. Before the fight, he stashed Rocky in a hotel with Goldman, then went to have dinner at Lew Tendler's, a restaurant owned by a former boxing champion, who drew the fight mob to his place on such nights. "The champeen of the world is fighting tonight," Weill told all his pals who happened by. "Louis? Nah, that's now. The next champeen, my boy, Rocky Marciano."

In the dressing room that night, Louis walked in. "Say, Joe," said Weill, "I want you to shake hands with my heavyweight." The affable champ nodded agreeably to the youngster. Later, Rocky recalled, "Joe stuck out his hand and we shook. He looked like a mountain and he had on a big, beautiful overcoat and a hat with a feather. I figured that hat alone must have cost fifty dollars, and now I got to thinking about all that dough."

Rocky gave the fight crowd and fans of Philadelphia and

his own manager their first look at him that night. He was awkwardly built and hard to fit. The legs of his baggy trunks were too wide and too long, and some suggested he looked like a burlesque comedian impersonating a fighter. Here in Philadelphia, where he'd win his title later, the crowd ridiculed him as he fought earnestly, but clumsily, in the ring. However, in the second round he connected and Ferron was finished. Still, the boxing crowd were not convinced that this new fighter had any real quality. That night they teased Weill about his "champeen." Charlie Goldman shrugged, "He may not look pretty, but he looks better than those other guys flat on their back." To Weill, he whispered, "Let them laugh. We'll have the last laugh."

Still, Weill was worried. His worries weren't eased any when Marciano came out of the fight with a fractured knuckle on his left hand. His hands had been hurting him all along, in and after every fight, and now he had to have a break repaired. Dr. Michael Del Colliano splinted the hand, later subjected it to heat treatment and physical therapy. He worked on both of Marciano's hands. Rocky laid off three months. He laid off real fighting. Goldman had him doing roadwork and shadowboxing in the gym. Goldman always liked shadowboxing as a good way to work with a fighter. He could get him to do things the fighter could not do in a ring when there was a foe who would not cooperate.

Rocky worried about his hands, too. He had finished his first full year as a professional with 12 consecutive knockouts, but he was getting hungry. He had been making $50, $75, $100 a bout, but he was not getting rich. Weill said,

"If they listen to me, they got a chance. I always get 'em top dollar. I get 'em as much as anyone could get for the class they're fighting. But I'm not gonna get 'em a quick buck. I'm not gonna get 'em a big fight for big money before they're ready. They got to be patient or they'll blow the big money at the end of the rainbow."

To Weill's credit, while he was stingy on expenses, he never cut Marciano in this period. While the Rock was battling preliminaries for short money, Weill let him keep it all. He still had to pay Goldman. He had to live. But he had his eye on bigger things.

World heavyweight champ Rocky with his friend and assistant trainer **Al Columbo** in May, 1953. *Wide World Photo*

4

Compassion and Carmine

In Rocky's first fight away from Providence, when he boxed Gil Cardione in Washington, he shared the same dressing room with Cardione. Before the bout, he and Cardione, a couple of earnest youngsters, got to talking and Cardione told him a hard-luck story of how tough things were for him at home.

"The poor guy's got nothing," Rocky whispered to Colombo. "I feel sorry for him."

"What have you got?" Colombo asked. "You can't feel sorry for him. He's an opponent. He's out there to hurt you."

"I knocked him out in one round," Rocky recalled later, "but I still felt sorry for him."

Fighting, hurting people, was alien to Marciano's nature, but it was his profession now, and if he was going to succeed in it he had to go out and do what had to be done.

Back home, his mother said, "I pray he no get hurt and the other boxer no get hurt. After all, the other boy has a mother too."

51

Barbara prayed for him too. Before each of his fights
she would take his boxing shoes to one of three priests in
their area to have them blessed. Then she would take them
to Rocky, tell him who had blessed them and wish him well.
He'd wear the "lucky" shoes in his bouts. After a while, he
realized that he seemed luckier with the blessings of one
priest than the others. "We always said we wanted the
one-round priest to bless the shoes," he laughed.

On March 21, 1949, he fought his first main event, and
apparently the one-round priest had not done the blessing,
because Johnny Pretzie lasted into the fifth round before
he succumbed. Rocky received $250 for this first feature
bout of his career, having graduated finally from the novice
ranks after a dozen straight victories in preliminary matches.
This was the first of six more bouts in a row in Providence
after his brief appearance in Philadelphia, and it proved his
hand was healed.

One week later, the one-round priest may have been on
the job because Artie Donato was knocked out in the first.
Two weeks later, Jimmy Walls fell in three. Then, three
weeks after that, Jimmy Evans fell in three. No one had
yet gone the distance with Rocky. But on May 23, Don
Mogard, an experienced pro, evaded Marciano's rushes, took
such punishment as he had to take and lasted the full 10
rounds with him. This ended Rocky's string of 16 consecutive knockouts, but it was his seventeenth straight victory as
a pro.

At this time, Al Weill was faced with a decision. The 20th
Century Sporting Club, under contract, had been promoting

all Madison Square Garden fights in New York City for a dozen years, since the fall of 1937. The owner, Mike Jacobs, had suffered a stroke, was aging and had fallen out of favor with General John Reed Kilpatrick and other officers of the Garden corporation.

A group called the Tournament of Champions had been organized by seven nonboxing men, including some show-business executives, to promote fights, including a series of Wednesday-night television shows on CBS, which had begun to rival NBC's Friday-night telecasts out of the Garden, and which wanted into the Garden.

Meanwhile, Joe Louis was ready to retire as heavyweight champion, but had tax problems and needed money. With his attorney, Truman Gibson, he arranged to form Joe Louis Enterprises, which would surrender the title if he could promote any elimination tournament to crown his successor and tie up the survivor.

Gibson sought to arrange a merger with the Tournament of Champions. He had a strong weapon with which to bargain. He had the heavyweight champion, and the organization that controlled the heavyweight champion could dominate boxing promotion. The Tournament of Champions was not succeeding, and those running it were interested in selling out, but they had invested a lot of money in their operation and wanted to get out with a profit.

Gibson and an associate, Harry Mendel, turned to Jim Norris and Arthur Wirtz, who owned or had controlling interest in the Detroit Red Wings hockey team, in the Detroit Olympia arena and the Chicago Stadium, and owned

around one third of the shares in Madison Square Garden.
Norris was interested in getting into boxing for the excitement of it and to fill his buildings.

He formed the International Boxing Club, which made
deals to buy out the 20th Century Sporting Club, and the
two years it had remaining on its Garden lease, and the
Tournament of Champions, for $100,000 each, while putting
Louis under long-term contract.

Harry Markson, who had been managing Garden boxing
for the 20th Century Sporting Club, was asked to continue to
do so for the IBC. He wanted Al Weill to be his matchmaker. Weill had been matchmaker for 20th Century. But
he once had insisted on $80,000 for an appearance by one of
his champions and so angered Jacobs that he eventually
fired Weill. However, Markson considered Weill the sharp-
est judge of boxing ability and styles in the business and
suggested to his bosses that Al could put together the most
interesting matches, which would return the most profits
at the least cost to the promoters.

Weill was offered the position, and he wanted it because
it would give him a good contract and considerable power.
However, New York State Athletic Commission rules fore-
bade matchmakers who managed fighters. Weill had
reached the point where he was reluctant to surrender
Marciano, but he was not sure Marciano would make it big
and he also was reluctant to turn down this new position.

His stepson, Marty, also was licensed as a manager, and
Al simply signed over "control" of Marciano to Marty and
became Garden matchmaker, while continuing to run

Rocky's career from behind the scenes. And he began to move him up in class, arranging stronger, more experienced opposition for him.

He still was not tackling the best heavyweights of that period, but Rocky could not learn much from or improve much with soft touches against outclassed opposition. "I don't want to put him in with someone too smart or with the style to beat him," Weill admitted. "I don't want him to get beat. But we got to take some chances." He was giving textbook demonstrations in the art of building up a fighter.

In mid-July, Rocky knocked out Harry Haft in three rounds. In mid-August, he took a rare trip, going into New Bedford, Massachusetts, to take out Pete Louthis in three. Then, back to Providence for three more fights. In late September, he flattened Tom DiGiorgio in four. Then, early in October, he took on Ted Lowry, had trouble with him and had to settle for a decision in ten rounds. Lowry had been around and he was a clever boxer and a determined man. He became the second fighter to last the distance against the heavy-handed Blockbuster from Brockton, but he could not beat him. It is significant that while he was no stylist, Marciano could force the action enough and land enough punches to get a decision over a good boxer. He did not have to knock him out to win.

Early in November, Marciano stopped Joe Domonic in two rounds, and Weill figured it was time to bring him into New York to give the local boys a sneak preview of his "phenom," who had won 22 straight bouts, 20 by KO! He booked him for $1,500 into a semifinal on the December 2 card at Madison Square Garden, Rocky Marciano's debut in the Big Town. He knocked out Pat Richards in two rounds.

Some were impressed by his strength and power, but some mocked his still-awkward style and some ridiculed his opposition. Goldman counseled, "Let them laugh at him. Rocky can hit and he can take a punch. He lives clean and he can fight forever. He fights the tough punchers and don't get hurt and knocks them out, and he fights the clever boxers and knocks most of them out, too, or at least beats them bad enough to get the decision."

Rocky returned to Providence to knock out tough veteran Phil Muscato in five rounds two weeks later, tuning up for his biggest test. Weill booked him back into the Garden eleven days later, on December 30, for a semifinal against Carmine Vingo, of the Bronx, a young knockout artist who would turn twenty years of age on that night. Vingo was beginning to attract attention as a young heavyweight of potential, and Weill was sufficiently anxious that no other prospect steal the spotlight from his boy to gamble, on Goldman's advice, that Marciano was about ready to move and could handle this other kid.

It was a sensational fight which the press later praised as one of the most exciting of the year. At first, Marciano moved right out and almost ended it quickly. He floored Vingo for a count of nine in the first round and again for a count of nine in the second round; but the Bronx boy was tough and determined and he got up each time, and in the third round began to rally and in the fourth round landed a left hook to Marciano's jaw which really hurt him, caused his knees to wobble, almost dropped him and almost beat him.

Marciano later admitted, "It was the hardest single punch I ever felt, even though I didn't go down. It really shook me and I felt it for several rounds afterward, as well as other hard punches he landed."

The bout became a brawl which had the big crowd in the old Garden on its feet and roaring. Normally, sophisticated New Yorkers take semifinals in stride, but this slugfest between two hard-hitting heavyweights had the nearly 10,000 fans wild. Marciano rallied in the fifth and began to punish Vingo heavily, though "Bingo," as his neighborhood admirers called him, kept battling back. In the sixth round, a short left hook crashed against Vingo's jaw and sent him collapsing to the canvas in a pile of pain.

The referee had counted as far as "three" when he decided he did not like the look on Vingo's face as he lay on the floor. He immediately waved both arms in the air, indicating he had stopped the fight right then and there as a knockout victory for the standing fighter, and waved the Garden physician, Dr. Vincent Nardiello, into the ring to take a look at the fighter.

As Nardiello hurried through the ropes, Vingo tried to rise, but fell back, unconscious. The doctor swiftly determined his injury might be serious and called for a stretcher so the youngster could be rushed by ambulance to nearby St. Clare's Hospital for extensive examination and treatment, if necessary.

Athletes have been and will continue to be killed in

all contact sports, primarily from head injuries. Protective equipment prevents most serious injuries, but in sports in which athletes must take hard blows of one sort or another there will be injuries or deaths from time to time. This is especially true in boxing, where the fighters wear padded gloves but are in the ring to hit their foes and to knock them out, if possible. Most fighters get cut and some are injured. Some have been killed from ring blows.

Like auto-race drivers, boxers understand that there are risks involved in their profession and they enter the ring of their own wishes not forced by anyone to continue in the cruel sport. Yet, most hope and assume accidents will not happen to them and simply try not to think about it. Marciano said later it never really occurred to him that he might seriously hurt someone as well as be seriously hurt himself, and it shook him as nothing else in his life apparently ever had.

For all of the violence with which he fought, which was the only way he was geared to fight effectively, he was a gentle, soft-hearted, compassionate person, who was visibly frightened by what he had done. In the hospital, he found Vingo's mother sitting in the corridor, weeping and waiting. "I just stood there and looked at her," he said. "I said, 'I'm sorry.' She didn't say anything."

He waited through the long hours and later admitted he vowed that if Vingo did not recover, he would retire from the ring. He considered doing that, anyway. The priest who gave Vingo last rites sought to console him, which the religious Rocky appreciated, but he was beyond consolation.

Associates and friends branded it an accident, but Rocky would not accept this.

Vingo had a fractured skull, a brain concussion and a blood clot on his brain. For forty-eight hours, Vingo hovered between life and death. Marciano could not sleep and haunted the hospital. Then Vingo began to rally. Gradually, his condition improved and he regained strength and consciousness.

Marciano donated his purse of $2,000 to Vingo to help pay for his hospital care. Later, he sent Vingo a $500 check to help him get started in a business. Vingo was partially paralyzed and never fought again. And Marciano never forgot this fight, though he went on fighting. Later, when Rocky married, he brought Vingo and his wife to Brockton as his guests. He became Vingo's friend, always ready to help him whenever needed.

This was Marciano's worst experience in boxing and the closest he came to leaving the ring before he retired seven years later. But once the crisis passed, it was back to boxing. He may have been sorry he was a boxer, but that's what he was, and it had helped him flee poverty and promised him riches. He could only hope that what had happened to Vingo would not happen again. And it did not in his career.

As 1949 ended, Rocky Marciano had completed two full years as a professional fighter with 25 consecutive triumphs, 23 by knockout. Once Vingo began to recover, the press turned its attention to his conqueror. It had been a wild fight and left Marciano, most reluctantly, branded as "a killer." In a curious and sad way, it added to his reputation.

He was a tough kid who could hit. But he really was no kid; he was twenty-six and it was time he showed what he really had.

Joe Louis had last defended his title in June of 1948. He had announced his retirement in March of 1949. Walcott, Louis' last victim, had been matched with Charles to determine a successor to the vacated crown, and Charles had won, then knocked out former light-heavyweight champion Gus Lesnevich in August and Pat Valentino in October to defend his new laurels.

There were not many good heavyweights around, and there was talk that Louis, who was continuing to box in exhibitions on tour—more than fifty of them from his last real fight through the end of 1949—might abruptly end his retirement to challenge the new king. In the meantime, there was considerable interest in the new prospects developing as potential challengers for the championship in the next few years. One of these now, suddenly, was Marciano. Another was Roland LaStarza, a former City College of New York student, and a brilliant boxer from the Bronx.

Marciano was in a good position. The new IBC hungrily eyed him as part of its fat future. The IBC's matchmaker, Weill, managed him behind the scenes. But those at the IBC who managed Weill wanted him to match Marciano with LaStarza in an elimination match that figured to draw a big gate of around $50,000. The IBC bosses were prepared to go ahead with LaStarza instead of Marciano if Roland could beat Rocky. In any event, the match seemed a "natural."

Weill was pressed to make the match. Marciano could be offered $5,000, by far his biggest purse. Weill was interested in this kind of money, but he was worried about LaStarza, who he figured might be too clever and skillful for his awkward tiger.

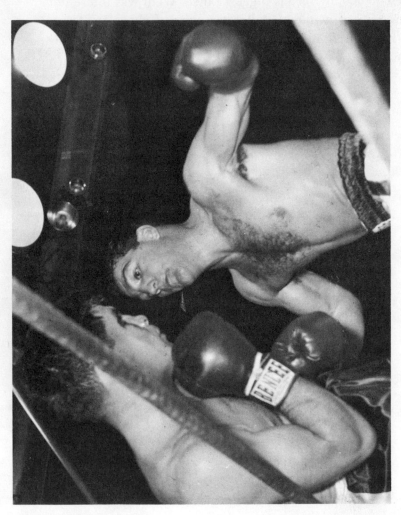

Rocky backs Roland LaStarza against the ropes in their second match in September, 1953. *United Press Photo*

5

Rollie and Barbara

After his next-to-last fight in 1949, a mid-December knock-out of Phil Muscato in Providence, Rocky Marciano was driving back to Brockton with pals Allie Colombo, Nicky Sylvester and Snap Tartaglia. Allie was driving. The powerful future champion never had learned how to drive a car.

Usually, the boys would be loudly joking and laughing as they drove home through the night after another knockout victory by their buddy; but now everyone was quiet and seemed serious, and Marciano recalled later that he sensed a difference this night. He soon found out what was on the boys' minds.

One of them said, "You know, Rock, you haven't got very far to go now."

And Rock said, "To go where?"

"For the title," one of them said.

"Ah, take it easy," Rocky said, surprised and embarrassed.

"No," one said. "Figure it out. About five or six good wins and you can be on top of the heap."

So this was what they had been talking about while waiting for him to change back into street clothes and join them at the car.

Together, they started to figure the fighters who stood between Marciano and a title shot: LaStarza, who was considered the best young prospect around. Rex Layne, a tough young brawler from the Pacific Northwest, who was considered another strong prospect. Maybe Jimmy Bivins or Lee Savold, a couple of veterans. Old Joe Walcott, who had been beaten in June by Ezzard Charles in a bout for the heavyweight title vacated by Joe Louis. Maybe Louis, if he came back. And Charles, the reigning champ.

They drove quietly and thoughtfully through the darkness to Rocky's house and dropped him off there. That night he had a hard time falling asleep. He recalled later, "I was a kid who never dreamed he could be heavyweight champ. I had dreamed of being a major-league catcher. I began to box because it was something I could do, but I didn't think I was championship good. Then I won and won and won. Now, I started to think what it would be like if I could be champion. I thought, 'Boy, when you're the heavyweight champion of the world it means you can lick any man in the world.'"

He remembered seeing and touching Primo Carnera and how big he looked. He thought of meeting Joe Louis and how big he looked. He fell asleep, finally, dreaming impossible dreams.

He was not without his troubles. A suit had been filed against him by Gene Caggiano, who claimed he had been Marciano's manager in his early period in the ring and by rights should remain as manager now of this young fighter who might become a champion. Marciano, who had always demonstrated his loyalty to his friends and his fairness, protested that Caggiano really had no right to such claims. It was up to the courts to decide the case, which dragged on through appeals as Caggiano's attorneys dueled attorneys hired by Weill for Rocky.

Weill was not about to surrender his position gracefully. But Caggiano did win a decision and a $30,000 settlement which the Massachusetts Supreme Court reversed in favor of Rocky. However, Rocky did not know this throughout 1950, since the case carried through the courts slowly, and he was disturbed by it.

He also was worried about his back. In August, before his bout with Pete Louthis in New Bedford, he had begun to feel a backache. His back was stiff and sore. He did not tell Al or Marty Weill or Charlie Goldman because he was doing so well; he did not want to worry them and he figured it would pass. But he did tell Allie Colombo and some of his buddies, warning them not to say anything to others. Against Louthis, the aching back made Rocky a bit more awkward than usual, but he was so awkward anyway no one noticed and he did what he had to do and took Louthis out in three. Afterward, Colombo had to help Rocky into his street clothes.

Everyone thought it was just a muscle strain which would

get better with some heat treatments and massage, but it persisted. In October he went to Al Norling, Health Director of the Brockton YMCA, who turned him over to Dr. Thomas Quigley of Boston. Rocky had x-rays taken that month and again the next month. They revealed nothing serious.

But x-rays are not alway revealing in the case of back injuries, which are difficult to detect. Rocky apparently had suffered some strain to his back, which lingered. Still, he could bear it since it didn't really bother him too much, and he decided to just go on with it. He swore Norling and Quigley to secrecy and never told his management.

Jim Norris wanted a Marciano-LaStarza match for his new IBC. He directed Al Weill to make it. Al said, "I'm not sure my boy is ready for it."

Norris asked, "Are you working for us or for him?" He said, "The match is ready to be made. Make it."

Weill made it, giving Rocky $5,000, his best purse to that point, with Weill to get half. Rocky was pleased, because now he was beginning to think of moving up to a championship chance and he wanted more prominence and more money than he had gotten so far. He felt he could beat LaStarza, and why not? Hadn't he beaten everyone he'd faced so far? He didn't know what it was to lose.

He told Weill, "I'm glad I got this match."

Weill turned on him, saying sharply, "You're glad? Who got this match? I got it. What are you? You're just the fighter. Without me, you're nothing." Another time, he said, "You have to watch out for these young, broke fighters."

Rocky said, "He told me what to eat, what to drink, what to read, who to talk to, when to go to bed, when to get up."

Twenty-six years old, Rocky did not like such close supervision and, of course, he did not have to take it. But he respected what a top manager could do for a fighter. He was afraid Weill might turn on him if he crossed the boss, and he seemed to be making such progress he was afraid of rocking the boat. Anyway, being run by a manager seemed to be the way it was with boxers, and it was the only way Rocky knew since he turned pro. So he accepted it.

Barbara had to accept it, too. Rocky and Barbara had been going steady since they met at a dance in Brookeville, Massachusetts, in 1947. She was working as a telephone operator. Soon, Rocky and she began to discuss marriage. They were both in their middle twenties, and it was time that they settled down and raised a family, if they were going to have one, which they both wanted. But Rocky wasn't making enough money yet and he was busy learning to box. He gave her an engagement ring and they waited.

He recalled later, "Her friends began to ask her when she'd get married, so she began to ask me and I began to ask Al." They did not need Weill's permission, but Rocky did not want to make such a move without his manager's consent. And Weill was not eager to give his permission. He was uninterested in a fighter's private life so long as it did not interfere with his ring career, and he was convinced women and marriage interfered. So was bachelor Goldman. Weill didn't want the fighter to be loyal to a wife instead of to him, to be advised by a wife instead of by him. He didn't want the fighter to be worried about a wife and family instead of his career.

Weill told Rocky, "Take it easy. You're just learning. Fighter's wives hurt fighters. When I think you're ready to get married, I'll tell you."

Rocky would get home from a fight and Barbara would ask, "Did you see Al? Did you ask him?" And Rocky would tell her what Weill said and she'd get mad. One time she called Weill, so she could speak to him, herself, and he "soft-soaped" her, saying, "Barbara, I've been a manager all my life and I know best. As soon as the right time comes, I want you kids should get married." Reluctantly, she accepted this. Rocky respected Weill's wisdom, so she had no choice. And she really didn't want to interfere with Rocky's ring progress. So they waited.

Rocky's biggest test was coming up, on March 24, 1950, in Madison Square Garden, his first big-time main event, against LaStarza. Marciano had not fought for three months. Weill had waited to make sure Rocky's mind was clear of the near-tragedy of the Vingo fight. Vingo was all right now. That was past. The future beckoned. Rocky trained hard for LaStarza, under Goldman's counsel.

Some 13,658 fans paid $53,723 to see the bout, which stole some spotlight from other sporting events in the newspapers and on radio and TV. The fight itself was televised. Millions watched. Here were two young heavyweights, one of whom might make it to the top.

LaStarza was 37–0 with 17 knockouts. Marciano was 25–0 with 23 knockouts. Rocky was the harder hitter, but La-

Starza was the classier boxer and some felt he had met finer opposition. LaStarza was younger, at 23, but more experienced. He went into the ring a slight favorite with the bettors. Most assumed Marciano would have to score a knockout to win and doubted he could stop the rugged, broad-shouldered collegian, who at 187 pounds outweighed Marciano by almost four pounds.

LaStarza also was taller and had a longer reach. From the opening bell, he outboxed Marciano, jabbing him effectively and keeping him off balance. When Marciano threw wild punches, LaStarza counterpunched effectively. Rocky seemed reserved at first, unable to let loose as freely as he had before the Vingo fight. It was as though it haunted him. For three rounds, Rocky fought awkwardly and ineffectively as the crowd jeered him and LaStarza outboxed him, putting his big gloves on Marciano's face.

Worried, Goldman pleaded with Rocky to get going. In the fourth round, a long right hand reached LaStarza on the side of his head and jarred him. He blinked and stepped back a second, then began to box more carefully than he had before. Now he suspected Marciano really could hit. Another long right reached LaStarza on the side of his head and jarred him.

As time was running out in the round, a long right by Marciano connected on LaStarza's jaw and he went down as though rammed by a pile-driver. The crowd roared to its feet. However, the punch had not landed squarely. Stunned, LaStarza shook his head as though to clear it and began to rise. He was resting on one knee at the count of eight when the bell rang.

Between rounds, Goldman instructed Marciano to go for the finisher, while LaStarza's handlers nervously pleaded with him to stay away from Marciano until his head cleared. The bright youngster tried. He jabbed from long range in the fifth and tied up Rocky with his arms when they came in close and wound up clinching. Rocky landed a couple of heavy right hands, which shook LaStarza, but he could not connect with a really big punch.

Gradually, LaStarza began to regain his bearings and rallied. In the sixth and seventh rounds, he outboxed Rocky again. Marciano had let him get away, off the hook.

The eighth round degenerated into a brawl. Punching furiously, Rocky landed one of his blows low, beneath LaStarza's waist, and at the end of the round the referee took the round away from Marciano on a foul and instructed the two judges to do the same. Later, all agreed Rocky had won the round otherwise, so losing it on a foul cost him heavily.

By now it figured to be a close decision. In the New York system, the referee and the two judges were scoring the fight by rounds and points, with the points to be used only if the round scoring came out even. Rocky had gradually been overcoming LaStarza's early lead, but now he had lost ground.

In the ninth and tenth, Marciano worked furiously to take out LaStarza, but he could not reach him with a finishing blow. Many of Rocky's blows went wild. Still, the rugged, durable, seemingly tireless New Englander overpowered the New Yorker, who boxed effectively and landed an occasional strong punch, but obviously was tiring.

At the final bell, the crowd rose to cheer the two youngsters who had given them such a spirited contest. No one was sure who had won, though the writers at ringside generally had scored the fight slightly in LaStarza's favor, as a poll of them later revealed. The two fighters waited worriedly as the officials' slips were turned in and counted, then turned over to announcer Johnny Addie.

Addie went to the center of the ring and pulled down the microphones. "Ladies and gentleman," he said. "Judge Arthur Schwartz scores it five rounds for Marciano, four for LaStarza, one even." The crowd roared in disagreement. Continued Addie, "Judge Artie Aidala scores five rounds for LaStarza, four rounds for Marciano and one even." The crowd roared again. Now the fighters each had a vote.

It was up to the referee's card. Addie said, "Referee Jack Watson scores five rounds for Marciano, five for LaStarza." The crowd hollered and Addie paused before concluding. "In points," Addie said, "he scores six points for LaStarza, nine for Marciano. The winner . . ." And the noise of the crowd drowned out his last words.

The winner, by an unusually narrow margin, was Rocky Marciano. Rocky was so relieved tears brimmed in his eyes. Charlie Goldman raised his fighter's hand triumphantly. LaStarza's crew stormed around angrily, his manager Jimmy (Fats) DeAngelo complaining bitterly to anyone who would listen that "We were robbed." The crowd seemed divided.

LaStarza's followers—there were more of them there in New York then—booed unhappily and threw debris at the ring. Marciano's supporters, fewer in number, cheered.

In the dressing room, Weill congratulated Marciano, who sat sweating and sore and weary and victorious, his unbeaten string intact. He had not knocked out LaStarza, but perhaps he had done better by outpointing a good boxer. Few had thought he could win without a KO. This, of course, was nonsense. The heavier hitter may not land enough punches or the right punches to flatten his foe, but he may land enough to outpoint even a superior boxer.

Flushed with triumph, sighing with relief, feeling charitable, Weill, in his official role of IBC matchmaker, went to LaStarza's room to congratulate him on his great effort. Wild with rage, DeAngelo slammed the door in Weill's face.

This was an act of anger, an error of judgment which was to cost DeAngelo and his tiger, LaStarza, heavily. This was a fight that was discussed controversially in the press and over the airwaves and in public places and private homes for days and weeks and months, and which many remember vividly to this day. It was, as it turned out, a truly important fight in the annals of boxing. And there was a great demand for a rematch. The IBC wanted it. And LaStarza wanted it. And even Marciano wanted it, feeling he could beat LaStarza more decisively and better prove himself. But Weill did not want it. Not even for five or ten times the $5,000 they'd been paid for the first fight.

Now Weill realized for sure he might have a future champion and he did not want to make a mistake with him. He pointed out as much to his IBC bosses, who reluctantly saw the wisdom of his reasoning. Marciano was arriving late. He had landed with one good punch which had turned the tide of battle in his favor this time, but he might not land one the next time, especially if it came too soon. In time, he'd take LaStarza apart. But give him time.

He had beaten LaStarza; there was not enough to gain in beating LaStarza again to risk losing to him. In time, the controversy would die down. The record would remain firm. Rocky was the winner. He could be built up much better than LaStarza, anyway. Marciano was a big hitter and LaStarza wasn't. Rocky was a crude but colorful brawler who could pump life back into the precious heavyweight picture, which had been dulled by Louis' retirement.

So there was no rematch then. Weill, who had been insulted by LaStarza's manager, felt no sympathy for them. He had his own fighter to worry about.

Rocky accepted Weill's decision. He went back to work. After a ten-week layoff from competition, he returned to the ring on June 5 back in Providence against Eldridge Eaton, whom he stopped in three rounds. There were only 4,183 fans on hand and the gate receipts were only $8,865. The press and public still had not accepted Marciano completely.

Weill booked Rocky into Boston, figuring the Brockton Blockbuster should show in New England's biggest city. He took a chance on him with Gino Buonovino, who was far from outstanding, but was big and tough and had been around, Weill deciding Rocky needed some sort of a "name"

foe to draw the crowd. Only 4,900 showed up and the gate
was only $11,188. And Buonovino punished Marciano some
and lasted into the tenth round before he succumbed.

Back to Providence, for his next four fights, three before
the end of 1950. After another ten-week layoff to recover
from the Buonovino ordeal, Marciano took on journeyman
Johnny Shkor, taking him out in six rounds. Two months
later, he was booked for a rematch with tough, talented Ted
Lowry, who had gone the ten-round distance with him
thirteen months earlier. This one drew 7,155 fans, the best
Marciano had yet done in his adopted "hometown." And
again Lowry went the distance with him, though again
Marciano won the decision.

Some years later, Marciano said, "Lowry was smart and
clever and tough. He went the distance with me twice, and
I think if I had fought him for the title he'd have gone the
distance with me again. I could beat him, but I couldn't get
to him to knock him out. I think maybe he could have gone
the distance with me everytime we fought."

But Lowry could not beat him, nor had anyone else Marciano had fought. His prestige was rising, his bank account
was growing, and his problems with Barbara also were increasing. Al could see they would not wait much longer, and
if they were to get married he'd better give his consent.
Grudgingly, hanging on as long as he could, Weill said, "One
more fight, OK?" Rocky said OK. Barbara said OK. Maybe
they'd break up before that one more fight. They did not,
nor would they ever. They were two people deeply in love.

The one more fight was on December 18 against Bill Wilson. Barbara was already making plans with her family and with Rocky's family for a big wedding on the last day of the year. Rocky did not want to get hit on the face or cut up and spoil his appearance for his wedding day. He determined to finish Wilson swiftly, which he did. Wilson went out in the first round.

Two days later Rocky went to Weill, who finally said all right. "Boy, was I happy," Rocky said. So was Barbara, although Weill told her, "You got to promise me you won't bother my fighter." She promised, not really wanting to disturb his career, ready to do anything to wed her man.

Weill asked Rocky what kind of a family he had in mind.

"A big one," Rocky smiled.

"Kids and fighters don't mix good," Weill warned, upset. "A big family keeps a fighter tied down too much. He should only have fighting on his mind."

Rocky nodded, shrugging. He didn't want to cross Weill, but he didn't want to cross Barbara either. They both loved kids and family life. He knew he did not want to have to wait too long before having his first child, anyway. After that, they would see.

The Rev. Leroy Cooney married them in St. Colman's Church in Brockton. The normally conservative Marciano was willing to go all out to make it a memorable occasion for his bride, their families and their friends. Some 650 persons had received invitations—about 800 showed up. Rocky spent his entire purse, $2,500, or at least his share of it, from the LaStarza fight, on the reception party later.

It was a memorable party, especially for Rocky, who did

not smoke or drink and was not given to extravagant affairs. He had Carmine Vingo and his wife there as his honored guests. The Ward Two boys had taken up a collection and presented him with a 1951 DeSoto, a brand-new car at that time and the first car Rocky ever had owned. He couldn't drive, but he had a car now.

Weill and Goldman were there, sorry to see their prize slipping into the hands of a woman. It was Weill's first visit to Brockton, and at dinner he showed his style when he arose to propose a toast to the newlyweds, then made a short speech. "Remember, Barbara," he said. "Rocky's boxing future comes first. You will have to play second fiddle because he'll have to pay strict attention to me." Everyone laughed, wanting Rocky to succeed in the ring, including Barbara, who was not comfortable, but Weill was in earnest, and she knew it and Rocky knew it.

Their friend Russ Murray, owner of the Raynham Dog Track, turned over his Easton estate to Rocky and Barbara as a temporary home, though they later moved in with her parents for a while before getting a home of their own. First, they went to Miami for a honeymoon. "Weill promised us a ten-day honeymoon," Marciano later laughed, "but he cut it down to seven days, and in that time he phoned me three times."

At the end of one week during which Weill and Goldman fretted over the soft life their tiger must be leading, Weill called Rocky to tell him a fight had been arranged with Keene Simmons in Providence for January 29 and Rocky would have to cut short his honeymoon and return east to resume training. Rocky protested, but Weill prevailed. It was important, Weill insisted. Rocky was hot now and he had to stay sharp. Big things loomed just ahead, he promised.

Joe Louis lay ahead.

Rocky with his wife Barbara and their eleven-month-old daughter, Mary Ann, November, 1953. *United Press Photo*

6

Rex and the Brown Bomber

Joe Louis, born in Alabama and reared in Detroit, turned professional in 1934 and had won 27 straight fights, 23 by knockout, before he was upset by Max Schmeling in June of 1936. Schmeling, a former champion and a good fighter, was older and more experienced. Louis was a smooth fighter, but there were flaws in his defense. Throughout his career, he was easy to hit and knock down, though hard to knock out. However, Schmeling hit him often, hurt him badly and stopped him in 12 rounds.

A precious property to Mike Jacobs' 20th Century Sporting Club, Louis was nursed back to prominence with seven straight wins. Meanwhile, Jimmy Braddock had come off the relief roles to upset playboy Max Baer for the heavyweight title in one of sports' most shocking reversals of form. Braddock's manager, Joe Gould, was Jewish and he did not want to give the German, Schmeling, a shot at the crown and the Nazis a hold on it. Louis was given the championship chance. He came off the canvas to stop Braddock in eight rounds.

Louis shuffled in and methodically took apart his opponents. During his rise to prominence, he knocked out two former champions, Primo Carnera in six rounds and Max Baer in four. By the time he became champion, most other fighters were afraid of him. They took bouts with him for big money, but were tense with terror until the finish. In contrast to most champions, who fight only once or twice a year, Louis set a record by defending his title 25 times. Only Tommy Farr, Arturo Godoy and Joe Walcott went the route.

Louis gave Schmeling a rematch in June of 1938 and knocked him out in two minutes and four seconds of the most savage display on the ring record books. In his next defense, he flattened light-heavyweight champion John Henry Louis in one round. In his next defense, he flattened Jack Roper in one round. In 1941, he defended his laurels six times in the first six months and knocked out each foe. He went into the Army for four years of his twelve-year reign. Two of these years, he did not defend his title. Twice he defended his title but gave up his purses to Army and Navy Relief Funds.

The first meeting between Jack Dempsey and Gene Tunney in September of 1926 in Philadelphia drew a record attendance of 120,757 fans and a gate of $1,895,733. The rematch in Chicago in September of 1927 drew 104,935 fans and a record gate of $2,658,660. Joe Louis and Billy Conn fit right in between the two Dempsey-Tunney bouts with their second fight, which drew only 45,266 fans, but at large prices for the second greatest gate of all time, $1,925,564. Louis was second only to Dempsey as an attraction in boxing history. He participated in two other million-dollar gates.

In the end, Louis earned $4,684,297 from gate, television and radio fees during his career, but he fell so far behind in income tax payments he never caught up. Even in retirement, the government hounded him, though he never was jailed, as an ordinary citizen might have been. The simple, modest, heroic Louis simply was too popular to be punished publicly.

Despite being knocked down by such as Tony Galento and Buddy Baer during otherwise one-sided matches, Louis really had trouble with only two foes during his long reign as champion.

Light-heavyweight champion Billy Conn outboxed him and had him outpointed after twelve rounds, but went for a knockout in the thirteenth and was, himself, knocked out in June of 1941. Because of the war, Conn did not get a rematch until June of 1946, when he was knocked out in eight rounds.

Joe Walcott floored Louis and appeared to outpoint him in December of 1947, but Louis was given a controversial decision. By then, Louis was thirty-three and slowing down. He gave Walcott a rematch in June of 1948 and knocked him out in eleven rounds. Louis was thirty-four and he did not defend his crown again.

While he continued to fight fifteen to thirty exhibitions a year from 1947 through 1951, the final five years of his career, Louis announced his retirement in March of 1949. Ezzard Charles gained recognition as heavyweight champion by outpointing Joe Walcott in an elimination bout in June. Louis came out of retirement to challenge Charles for the crown in September of 1950, but the Brown Bomber was rusty, slow and outpointed. But Louis felt he was still capable of regaining the title if he started again and worked himself up to it. He needed the money and the IBC wanted him as an attraction. So he continued to fight.

In November, Louis decisioned Cesar Brion in Chicago. In the first half of 1951, he knocked out Freddie Beshore in Detroit, Andy Walker in San Francisco and Lee Savold in New York and decisioned Omelio Agramonte twice, in Miami and Detroit. On tour, Louis was rebuilding his reputation and there were many who felt he could recapture his old magic.

Meanwhile, Marciano was marking time. He knocked out Keene Simmons in eight in Providence, Hal Mitchell in two in Hartford and Art Henri in nine in Providence. The end of April, he was taken the full ten rounds by a hit-and-run veteran, Red Applegate, in Providence. The newspaper writers were beginning to ridicule the record he was building in the shadows in Providence. Weill could see he could no longer afford to hide his boy out while building him up.

With 35 consecutive victories, 31 by knockout, Marciano's record was impressive, but the caliber of his opposition was not. The New York and nationally syndicated writers wanted to see him tested by fighters of quality, and the fans were clamoring for another look at him. It was suggested he be seen against Louis, which would be a good test for both of them. Either the young kid would prove he had it against the old man or the old man would prove he still had it. Actually, or course, Marciano was no kid. He was twenty-eight years old now, and after three and one half years of development it was time to make a big move with him. Still, Weill was wary of Louis, perhaps still dazzled by Joe's glamour.

Another hot young heavyweight had come along, Rex Layne, in whom Jack Dempsey had an interest, which added to the attractiveness of the newcomer. Layne was a big, rough kid from Utah who had won 36 of 37 fights. And he had been tested, having upset old Joe Walcott in December of the preceding year. Still, Goldman reasoned that Rocky was rugged enough to handle another rugged kid and would be better off with a young brawler than a smart, seasoned veteran like Louis. He recommended to Weill that it would be a good match for Rocky, and Weill agreed.

The Marciano-Layne match was made for July in Madison Square Garden. To prepare for it, Rocky was taken to his first training camp, to Long Pond Inn on Greenwood Lake in upstate New York. Here, far from the busy city, far from his wife and family, Marciano was dedicated to hard training. He ran long miles down country roads, worked hard rounds in the ring with sparring partners. He was told to think of nothing but Rex Layne. Goldman, who had worked Cesar Brion's corner in a loss to Layne, told Rocky that if he stayed on top of Layne and forced him back steadily, the Utah boy gradually would give way.

Ten days before the bout, a Superior Court judge reversed the earlier ruling and declared that Gene Caggiano had no claims on Marciano. Gaining this verdict probably gave Rocky some sort of a mental lift. He did not like the messiness of such a public dispute and was relieved that it was over and that he had won.

He needed all the help he could get. It is probable that his camp underestimated Layne, though by now they had no choice but to take on top fighters if they hoped to gain a championship chance for their boy. In any event, Layne proved an exceptionally tough foe.

A crowd of 12,565 came to see the televised ten-rounder, bringing Rocky another $25,000. He earned every dime of it. It was hailed by the press the next day as one of the most savage battles ever fought.

The pale Layne, who entered the ring a 1-2 favorite, bore in and mauled Marciano in the midsection, banging him heavily around the ribs, for two rounds, while Rocky head-hunted, missing more of his wild swings than he landed. In the second, the two bumped heads, and Layne bled from a cut above his left eye the rest of the way.

In the third round, Marciano heeded Goldman's advice to turn to a body-attack, too, and the two worked on each other's bodies in close, furiously, while the crowd stood and urged them on. In the fourth, Layne began to give ground. As he dropped his guard to protect his midsection, Marciano resumed firing for his foe's head. A right to the jaw knocked Layne down and brought the fans up, screaming, but Rex rose and carried on.

Both were showing rare courage, but no matter how heavily he landed, Layne could not seem to hurt Marciano, while Marciano seemed now to be hurting Layne. In the fifth round, Marciano hit and hurt Layne frequently as the two stood toe-to-toe slugging it out and thrilling the crowd. By the end of the round, Layne seemed exhausted and unsteady.

The bell rang for the sixth round. The two fighters moved out of their corners at each other. They moved around warily for almost half a minute. Suddenly, Marciano saw an opening and let his right hand go. He was in close to Layne and it was a short punch, traveling perhaps six inches. He had learned his lessons well. All the weight of his body was behind the blow.

Layne began to fold up, sinking slowly into a bent position until he was kneeling with his head down and his gloves on the canvas. The referee, Mark Conn, counted over him. Later, Layne said, "I heard the numbers from one to ten and I kept telling myself I had to get up, but I couldn't move."

When the count reached ten, Marciano jumped for joy, and many of his fans tried to get into the ring to congratulate him. He was given what James P. Dawson of *The New York Times* later described as "one of the most tumultuous demonstrations ever accorded a fighter." For twenty minutes the Garden was in an uproar as the fans cheered their new favorite.

At that instant, Rocky Marciano truly caught on with the public. Suddenly now, everyone clamored to see this new sensation who disdained the science of the manly art and crashed through defenses to brawl his way to victories— dark hair flying, dark eyes glistening, hard, broken face grimacing as he punched, sometimes sticking out his tongue comically with the extreme effort of his punches. He was regarded as a new Dempsey, which boxing badly needed.

Ezzard Charles was a brilliant stylist, but he was no tiger and lacked crowd appeal. In July, he gave Jersey Joe a rematch in Pittsburgh and was nailed on the jaw by a single punch in the seventh round which knocked him out and made old Walcott a stunning upset winner and the surprise new heavyweight champion of the world. By contract, Charles was entitled to a return match. The heavyweight title was tied up between the two of them for a while, which made a Marciano-Louis match more logical than ever.

On August 1, Louis outpointed Cesar Brion in San Francisco. On August 15, he decisioned Jimmy Bivins in Baltimore. The IBC leaders were on hand in Baltimore and they were unimpressed by Louis' form. Now Marciano seemed a hotter property to them. They were ready to feed the old lion to the young tiger in pursuit of future profits.

Louis seemed reluctant to face Marciano, however. He wanted Walcott again, or Charles if he regained the title from Walcott. Louis seemed to feel he had less to fear from them. However, he had to stay in the spotlight and he was offered Marciano. For this match, Louis demanded the lion's share of the profits, 45 percent of the 60 percent usually given the principals.

Meanwhile, Weill still was resisting the match. After returning to New York, IBS manager Harry Markson said to Weill, "Al, after seeing Louis, how can you turn him down for Marciano?"

Weill said, "I manage my own fighter."

Markson said, "Louis will be easy for Marciano."

"I manage Marciano, not you," Weill insisted stubbornly.

But he could not avoid the issue much longer. Even at 15 percent, he would make more money than he had been making with Marciano, and it was a chance to clinch prominence and all but wrap up a lucrative title shot for the following year. Goldman advised him Rocky was ready to overpower the aging Louis, and Walcott, too, for that matter. Charles might be another matter, but Charles was not the champion now.

In August, Weill took Marciano to Boston, where nearly 10,000 fans came to see the new sensation flatten Freddie Beshore in four rounds. Marciano wanted the best now. He was tired of waiting. Weill could see that. He made the Marciano-Louis match for October 26 in Madison Square Garden. It was a tremendously interesting attraction for the press and the public. The buildup boomed. Both fighters went into heavy training in camps.

Marciano's back still was bothering him. Dr. Gardner Bassett of Brockton examined him and found calcium deposits in the joints which had produced an arthritic condition. As Rocky fought, small tears had developed in the muscles of his back. As these healed, scar tissue formed. In

time, this scar tissue rubbed off and some of it remained
lodged in the joints, like flecks of salt irritating the muscles.
It is similar to conditions baseball pitchers develop in their
arms and basketball players in their knees. In Marciano's
case, an operation seemed out of the question. It might do
more harm than good. It was something he would just have
to learn to bear. He kept his secret from Weill and Goldman.

He entered the ring a slight underdog to Louis. Joe was
nine years older at thirty-seven. And he had been fighting
fourteen more years. He did have an obvious advantage in
experience, especially in big fights. He was a much bigger
man—heavier, taller, with a longer reach. He weighed 212
pounds and stood six feet one. Marciano was 187 and five
ten. Looking across the ring at Louis, Marciano was awed
by Joe's size and reputation.

There were 17,241 fans crammed into the triple-tiered
building, which seemed to Marciano to rise to the heavens.
Their noise poured over him. They had paid $152,845 to
see the match. TV and radio had paid more money. Millions were gathered in front of television sets across the
country. The stakes were high and the pressure enormous.

The house lights darkened, the bell rang and the fighters
moved out alone in that small, spotlighted squared ring.

Louis always had a left jab that was quicker, sharper and
heavier than most men's knockout punches. He also could
knock out a man with either hand if he was quick enough
to pour a big punch into such openings as developed. That
was the question now—that and whether he could take the

sort of punishment Marciano dished out with his relentless style.

From the first, Louis jabbed and jabbed and jabbed, breaking up Marciano's face. Later, Marciano recalled, "I couldn't avoid it. I just had to take it. My face was sore for a week after the fight."

Marciano kept trying to move in, throwing right hands, but most missed as Louis ducked and counterpunched. Midway in the first round, Louis chopped a right uppercut to Marciano's jaw which shook him. But just before the bell, Marciano staggered Louis with a right to the head. In the second round, Marciano hooked a left to the head and drove both hands to Joe's body, but Louis jabbed him away and drove left, right, left to Marciano's head. Most of the round, Louis kept jabbing Marciano away, but Rocky drew him into a two-fisted exchange near the bell and had the better of it.

In the third, Marciano jarred Louis with two lefts to the chin, but then missed with a right uppercut, grazing Joe's chin. A little later, he drove a long right to Joe's head, but then missed with a big right. Louis kept jabbing, jabbing, jabbing. He landed an occasional right, but mostly he was a one-handed fighter, a left-handed fighter, whose right would not respond in time when the chances came.

In the fourth, Louis jabbed powerfully and even hooked some to Marciano's head effectively. He made Marciano look bad in places. But Marciano kept coming. He dug a right to Joe's body which set up Joe for a right to the head, but Rocky missed with it. At the bell, Louis did land a hard right to Marciano's chin which jarred Rocky and showed him he was far from safe.

The crowd was tense and making a lot of noise, waiting for the seemingly inevitable explosion by the old warrior or the young tiger. In the fifth, Louis jabbed Marciano repeatedly, keeping him off balance, but he was late and long with a right aimed at Rocky's chin which curled around his head. At round's end, Louis landed two rights to Marciano's jaw, but they did no damage.

They had passed the halfway point now and Louis seemed to be tiring. In the sixth, Marciano moved right in past Joe's jabs, and his punches began to land consistently if not cleanly. Desperately, Louis began to pump both fists into Marciano's midsection, but he could not wear him down. At the bell, Marciano hit Louis with a long left and a long right, and the crowd roared.

In the seventh, Marciano began to land with left hooks as well as right crosses. Louis fought back desperately, but Marciano outpunched him. Louis tried to jab and Marciano jarred Joe with two lefts and a right to the jaw. Desperate now, Louis tried a left hook which landed and rocked Marciano at the bell, but Rocky did not go down.

At the bell for the eighth, Marciano charged out and threw a wild right to the head. Louis ducked it and tossed punches in return, but Marciano relentlessly bore in on the now-weary old warrior. Marciano was short with a left hand, but came back with a long right which landed on the side of Louis' head and hurt him badly. Joe's eyes seemed to glaze and his hands dropped. Marciano lunged at him with a left hook which banged Joe's jaw with the force of a battering ram, and Joe went down as the fans came up.

All was madness now in the Garden. Louis struggled up at the count of eight, exhausted and dazed, but trying his best. Marciano was on top of him, landing two left hooks. Louis stood helplessly with his arms dangling at his sides. Marciano threw a right hand which crashed into Joe's chin, and the ex-champ collapsed head-first through the ring ropes until he lay through them, half in and half out of the ring. Referee Ruby Goldstein signaled it was all over.

From the crowd, the great Sugar Ray Robinson rushed into the ring to kneel by Joe's side. After 71 fights, the golden career of the Brown Bomber had ended with his third loss, second by knockout.

Marciano jumped about in jubilation, then stopped. "I saw him laying there—a great fighter finished, and I remembered his greatness," he said later. "I just couldn't help feeling sorry for him." As Louis was helped to his feet, Marciano went to him to congratulate him on his effort and console him on his defeat. The crowd cheered.

In the dressing rooms later, the writers swarmed all over the two combatants. Louis' face was swollen and sore. He sat wearily on a dressing table, remembering better nights, winning nights, past glories. It was all over now. But he remembered to be gracious. "The better man won, that's all," he said. "I was too old, I guess." He paused and shut his eyes for a second. Then he shrugged and said, "This boy is tough enough to beat anyone."

Louis never fought again.

In his quarters, Marciano sat soaked with sweat, his face puffy and bloody and in worse shape than Joe's. He had won, so he was smiling, but it was hard for him to smile. The writers seemed to think it should be easy, as though boxers did not pay a heavy price for some victories. Marciano talked about what a great fighter Louis had been and how sorry he was to have been the one to have done this to Joe, but it was his job to do so he had done it.

Most fighters will not admit they have been hurt in a fight. Nor, losing a decision, will they admit they deserved to lose. Marciano insisted Louis had hurt him several times with punches and had been dangerous to the end. He said he was not sure he would have won the decision if the bout had gone the distance, so he had gone for the knockout. Knockouts were his style, anyway. But a check of the official cards showed he led 5-2, 4-2-1 and 4-3 at the finish.

They asked Marciano who he wanted next. He said, "The champion."

He seemed curiously sad, as though he had hurt on old friend. He showered and dressed and left quietly with an entourage of well-wishers whooping around him happily. Some hated him for having done this to Joe Louis, an idol of rare dimensions, but Joe's day was done, and it was Rocky's time now and he suddenly was a national hero and a great celebrity.

The sportswriter Jimmy Cannon went up to Marciano's hotel room the next morning. He wrote, "He was trying on his first tuxedo and the tailor was having a miserable time trying to make it fit that short-armed, squat, heavy-legged body." Marciano was uncomfortable in the new role which his ability had created for him. He was now a great, feared fighter.

**Rocky with President Eisenhower and Yankee slugger
Joe DiMaggio at a White House luncheon for sports
personalities, June, 1953.** *United Press Photo*

7

The Kid and Old Joe

Joe Walcott, the new heavyweight champion, was picking up loose change on the exhibition trail while delaying the rematch with Ezzard Charles, the ex-champ, until midsummer. A title shot for the new glamour boy of the heavyweights, Rocky Marciano, would have to wait until the fall, at least. Meanwhile, Rocky could not afford to grow rusty.

He laid off more than three months after his knockout of Joe Louis before Weill put him in with blond Lee Savold in Philadelphia. Savold had been a good fighter, but he was wearing out. He had been knocked out by Louis in six rounds the preceding June and he figured to serve as an excellent showcase for Marciano as Rocky opened his 1952 campaign in mid-February.

Savold was thirty-five, but smart and strong. Most figured Marciano would finish him fast, but they were disappointed. Already rust had begun to accumulate on Rocky and he looked clumsy—he *was* clumsy. Nearly 10,000 fans paid to see him show off and they hooted his efforts, and the writers ridiculed his performance.

Actually, Rocky landed enough right hands to deal Savold savage punishment, but he could not land cleanly enough to floor or knock out the veteran, and the fight ended with Savold sitting in his corner, unable to go on any further. The record books show it as a knockout in six, but memory reveals it as an unsatisfactory showing which did not add to Marciano's glamour.

What went unnoticed was that Savold in the dressing room afterward was a wreck, hardly able to speak. His lips were split and swollen and some of his teeth had been driven into his gums. He had to be hospitalized. He had stood up gamely under Marciano's wild attack, but he had paid a heavy price for it.

Determined to keep Marciano busy and sharp, Weill and Goldman booked him back into Providence in April with Gino Buonovino, whom Marciano stopped in two sessions, and in May with Bernie Reynolds, whom Marciano finished in three rounds. These were the last fights Marciano ever fought in Providence. Coming up, he had used this as his schoolroom for no less than 28 bouts.

In June, Walcott gave Charles the rematch, and while many felt Charles had outpointed the champion, Walcott got the decision. It was mildly controversial, but since Charles had not forced the action or scored heavily, few outside of his camp were upset about it. Walcott had fought a smart, careful fight, and Charles simply had not been aggressive enough to recapture his precious laurels. It was a dull fight between two masterful boxers who had not forced one another into unloading any heavy weapons.

More than ever now, the press and public clamored for the spectacular knockout artist Marciano to get his chance. They wanted a more exciting champion than they had. Meanwhile, however, a new name had risen to prominence, Harry "Kid" Matthews, an Idaho-born light-heavyweight who had settled in Seattle and had fought for some years without distinction before coming into the hands of Jack Hurley.

Hurley was acknowledged as one of the shrewdest of boxing men and an imaginative manager and promoter. He had taught Matthews a lot and built him up with a long series of victories over undistinguished opposition. He called Matthews "my athlete" and said he was a great one, the greatest to come along in years. While many regarded such claims dubiously, Hurley's shrewdness was so well regarded no one was willing to bet he had not developed a real terror.

Hurley once had been associated with Jim Norris, but had fallen out with Norris, and now Hurley claimed he and his boy were being blackballed by the IBC. He demanded a shot at light-heavyweight champion Joey Maxim. When he did not immediately get it, his cries of outrage stirred Idaho Senator Herman Welker and Washington Senator Harry Cain to demand an investigation of the IBC's monopoly on major boxing matches, which, it was claimed, had reduced the sport to "a new low."

Attorney General Howard McGrath ordered aide Melville Williams to launch a grand jury probe, which took testimony from boxing figures, but found nothing amiss. Meanwhile, Jack Kearns, who formerly managed Jack Dempsey and now managed Maxim, agreed to an IBC match with Matthews for the title, agreeing to let Matthews have 20 percent of the returns, which was as much as challengers ever get, but Hurley surprised everyone by turning it down. The senators withdrew their support and the investigation was ended.

Hurley by then had decided to gamble on bigger game. He had decided Matthews might not make merely light-heavyweight champion, but heavyweight champion. He wanted a heavyweight title fight for his athlete, which would return far more than a light-heavyweight shot.

Hurley continued his publicity campaign, calling attention to the fact that Al Weill, not Marty Weill, was the real manager of Rocky Marciano and that, by holding down a position as matchmaker of the IBC, he was violating New York State Athletic Commission rules. This had been discussed by newspaper writers in print but had not been acted on by the commission.

Angrily, Norris sought a solution in which he could, hopefully, get rid of Hurley and Matthews without having to give them a shot at the heavyweight title. Finally, he figured it out.

"Let's put Marciano in with Matthews," was his proposal to Weill.

"Not me. I don't want it," said Weill, who figured Marciano should be first in line for a Walcott match, anyway, and did not want to risk it with Hurley's fighter, whom he did not know and so feared.

"We need the match," insisted Norris. "Let's put the guy on the spot and figure out if Matthews can fight."

"Get somebody else," Weill said.

But Norris kept up the pressure, going to friends who had influence with Weill. Finally, Weill relented. He did not want to be shut out of a Walcott match. He had to take a chance and go along. The match was offered Hurley. He did not want it either. However, it was made clear to him that if he did not fight Marciano, he would not get to fight Walcott. And it also was clear to him that while not a championship fight, a bout with Marciano would be a big one, much bigger than a light-heavyweight title bout, and they'd all make a lot of money. Reluctantly, he agreed.

However, Hurley vetoed television. He felt Norris and the IBC were ruining boxing by giving away their matches on home television. He felt they were making money then, but would lose in the long run. And he figured that without TV, he'd get a bigger gate, which would more than make up for the lack of home-screen fees.

The match was made for July 28 in Yankee Stadium, New York, Marciano's first big outdoor ball-park spectacular. And it drew 31,188 fans to see the ballyhooed battle. Marciano still had not convinced some that he could reach a skillful performer, and the buildup Hurley had given Matthews convinced many that Matthews was a skillful performer, who could evade Marciano's bull-like charges and cut him to pieces with sharp punches. Many felt Marciano's undefeated record was about to be smeared.

"The Seattle Kid" boxed smartly for one round and won

it from the judges. However, just before the bell, Marciano landed a heavy punch which so dazed his pale, slim foe he started to go to the wrong corner when the round ended. Hurley did not realize how badly Matthews was hurt and he told him between rounds to "keep it up." Matthews never answered.

In the second round, Matthews jabbed as Marciano missed. Then Marciano moved inside the jabs and landed some heavy body blows, which caused Matthews to back up. As Matthews moved back, Marciano lashed out with a left hook which landed heavily on the side of the Kid's jaw. His eyes glazed and he started to sag. Before Matthews got far, while he was on the way down, Marciano unloaded another left hook which landed on the Kid's jaw with lethal effect.

Matthews was sent sprawling. His head hit the lower ropes and he rolled over and through the ropes, face down, where he lay as he was counted out. It was all over very fast. The crowd was on its feet, startled at the suddenness of the ending; they had started to scream, then seemed stunned for a while before according Marciano a great ovation. He had dispelled the myth of Matthews and cemented his hold on the fans' affections. And earned $50,000.

The morning of the fight, there had been the usual weigh-in, held in the Madison Square Garden lobby. Matthews was late. When State Athletic Commissioner Bob Christenberry asked Weill where Matthews was, Weill said, "How should I know? All I know is my fighter's here." It was his first public admission that he still managed Marciano. Combined with increasing newspaper comment about

Weill's dual status and the Hurley ridicule of the situation, Christenberry had to act. He called Harry Markson into his office and said, "The masquerade is over. If you don't have his resignation by tomorrow at this time, I will lift the IBC's license." Markson told Norris, who told Weill. Weill handed in his resignation.

No one was unhappy—not Norris, who was tired of having to argue with Weill over decisions, or Weill, who now realized what a hot property he had in Marciano. All along, Weill had been wary of moving Marciano up, but Rocky had hurdled each obstacle successfully. Now his camp wanted Walcott without reservation.

Walcott could have ducked Marciano for a while, but Jersey Joe was thirty-eight, and he wanted to cash in on his new title fast. If he fought someone else first, he might wind up losing to a lesser foe for lesser dough. If he gave Marciano his chance, it would be a big fight and Joe could name his own terms and make a bundle. And the clever Walcott was convinced he could handle the crude Marciano. "He can't fight," Joe sneered. "If I don't whip him, take my name out of the record books."

Walcott's camp demanded stiff terms. They asked 40 percent of the fighters' 60 percent for the match, plus a guaranteed return bout at the same percentages if they lost. They also wanted the fight in Philadelphia's Municipal Stadium, practically in the Camden veteran's backyard. Weill had no choice but to take Jersey Joe any way he could get him. The match was made swiftly for September 23. The fighters were isolated in camps and the buildup boomed.

By this time, Marciano had gained the respect of the experts. At twenty-nine, he had nine years' advantage over old Joe, and he was considered a far more powerful puncher. By ring-time, Rocky was a 3–1 favorite. However, Walcott was not without his supporters, who felt he was seriously underestimated. He was no youngster—the oldest man ever to hold the title—and he had been around, of course, though for many years he had trouble obtaining fights. In 23 years as a professional, Walcott had won 49, lost 15 and drawn 1 of 65 bouts. He had knocked out 30 men and been knocked out 4 times. However, most of his reversals came early in his career. In the last six years he had lost only to Louis, Layne and Charles. Most thought he had outpointed Louis and he had knocked out and outpointed Charles.

Walcott was an unorthodox but brilliant boxer and had power in both hands. And at 196 pounds he was 12 pounds heavier than Marciano.

Marciano remained undefeated as a pro, but no undefeated fighter ever had won the heavyweight championship. He had won 42 consecutive fights, 37 by knockout, and he had been forced to go ten rounds only five times in his career and never farther. This one was for fifteen if it went that far. Not only had he never been beaten, he had never even been knocked off his feet, but now he was up against a master stylist, far sharper than anyone he had ever faced, whom he perhaps underestimated.

In his training camp, at Grossinger's in upstate New York, Rocky talked as though he had already finished Walcott. He spoke now of gaining respect, perhaps attaining greatness.

He was dedicated to the ring, he said. "I'd like to be a man that people will remember," he said. "Like now it's Jack Dempsey and Joe Louis, and maybe someday it will be Dempsey, Louis and Rocky Marciano." In Walcott's camp, Joe smiled and said, "I gave up a lot of my life to get this title and I'm not going to give it up easy."

The fight was televised into fifty theaters in thirty cities across the country, the most extensive closed-circuit network yet arranged. Even drive-in theaters were carrying the bout for the first time. But there was no home television and no home radio broadcast. Many in Brockton went to the big cities to see the bout. Others gathered around the social club and the newspaper office to get wire reports. Lena Marciano, who had never seen or listened to any of her son's fights, went with two sisters to St. Patrick's Church to pray. Her husband, two younger sons, three daughters and Rocky's wife went to Philadelphia to see Rocky fight and were in the crowd of more than 40,000 people who paid more than half-a-million dollars to see the outdoor spectacle. TV had guaranteed another $125,000 to beam the show across the country. A dozen rows of reporters, typewriters clacking, peered up, pressing in at ringside.

As Marciano fidgeted in his corner in the cool night, he felt sick from the tension. As he said, "I wasn't afraid of fighting, only of losing." Old Walcott pranced around across the way, apparently cool and relaxed. He'd been there before. The great saucer was darkened, leaving only the ring spotlighted. The bell rang and the two fighters moved out to meet one another, alone in that roped square except for the referee watching them. The noise of the crowd washed over them.

"All the time you're getting ready for a fight, working hard, but relaxed, always surrounded by people, never alone," Rocky once said, "and then suddenly it's time and you go out there, you and the other guy, and you're all alone out there in front of all those people and you have to take what you've learned and use it without making any bad mistakes, because one slip and it might be all over and there might not be another chance. You don't think of the money, although that's what you're in there for. You don't think of the crowd, although sometimes you hear them. You're trying to concentrate. You have your pride. All you want to do is win. And it's just you and him and only one of you can win."

He went at dark, stern Walcott hard, right from the start, boring in, throwing those long, looping right hands, willing to take punishment, unafraid of Walcott. And Walcott surprised him by coming at him hard, trying to catch him off guard, hitting him in the first minute with a hard left hook to the jaw which landed so hard and so cleanly it dropped Marciano heavily to the canvas, where he'd never been before. He looked up at Walcott, startled, his eyes bleary, his legs curled underneath him, trembling, and he saw Joe strutting to a neutral corner. Rocky heard the referee counting and he pushed right up at "three." "I was more angry than hurt," he said later.

Perhaps he should have waited out a longer count, and perhaps Walcott should have come at him more aggressively to try to finish him, but Marciano wanted to make up for his mistake, while Walcott didn't want to make any mistakes. Joe felt more than ever now that he could beat this clumsy young fellow, and he was in no hurry. He boxed while Marciano bore in on him. He shook Rocky several times with heavy punches, but he did not launch an all-out attack. He waited for openings he was sure would present themselves. Rocky did not wait for openings. He did not panic, but he pressed in hard. He got through the round.

By the start of the second round, Rocky was in full command of his senses again. He went at Walcott hard, throwing mostly long, looping right hands and sidearm left hooks, trying to punish old Joe while looking for openings to throw short punches inside. Walcott moved around. His style was like a dancer's. He shuffled and did little steps and sometimes dropped his hands to his side and invited his foes to fire away at him while slipping and ducking punches with shifts of his head and shoulders. He fought with arrogance, moving in and out lightly, counterpunching heavily.

As Marciano missed punches, Walcott stepped inside them and countered them, his hands moving swiftly. Then he danced out of range again. The rounds slipped away from them: Round three. Round four. Round five. It was an even, tough fight. Walcott landed more often, but Marciano landed more heavily. Then, in the sixth round, their heads collided and Marciano was cut on his scalp and Walcott was cut over his left eye.

Their seconds worked on the cuts and neither got in trouble with them, though both were bloody from then on. However, Marciano's eyes began to burn and his vision got cloudy and he told his corner between rounds that something was getting into his eyes, irritating them and blinding him. Perhaps it was from medication applied to Marciano's cut scalp or medication applied to Walcott's cut eye which rubbed onto Marciano's face, or perhaps, as Weill screamed at the referee and opposing corner, from some ointment being rubbed on Walcott's gloves. No one ever found out. But everyone could see Marciano was bothered and having trouble seeing.

Still, he struggled on through the seventh and eighth and ninth and tenth rounds, in agony, but knowing no other way, punching wildly, hurting Walcott wherever he hit him, but not hitting him cleanly enough to put him down. And Walcott danced around him and boxed him, amazingly spry and tough for his age, and counterpunched him viciously. Several times, Joe hit him hard and clean, but he could not put him down again. Marciano just shook off the blows and kept wading in. But Walcott was winning the rounds now, building up a big lead, winning the fight, and the fans were screaming at the upset that was shaping up on this dark, cool, moist night.

Gradually, whatever had been getting into Marciano's eyes disappeared and his vision cleared up and the irritation stopped, but his face by now was red and bruised from punishment and he still could not catch Walcott. Rocky pressed the champion against the ropes with a left, a right and a left to Joe's head, but Walcott uncorked a powerful right hand to Marciano's jaw and then a lethal left hook, which rocked the challenger back on his heels as the crowd roared. A left hook split open the skin above Rocky's right eye, and the champion rocked him again with a tremendous left hook as the bell sounded, ending the eleventh round.

The crowd was screaming and Weill, nearly hysterical, was screaming louder than anyone else. It was getting away from them and they knew it. In the twelfth round, Rocky rushed at Walcott, punching wildly, but missing, and getting counterpunched. The pattern did not vary. Marciano missed with a looping left and took a short left hook to the jaw. Rocky missed with a wild right. He landed a left to the jaw, but Walcott drove a left hook to Marciano's belly which caused Rocky to gasp for breath and doubled him over for a second. A short left and right drove Rocky back a few steps. Then Rocky came on again. He kept coming on, coming on, coming on. The bell sounded.

Marciano had gone two rounds further than he had ever fought in his life before. He was weary. Walcott, the older man, was weary. But neither had slowed down. The stakes were high and they were waging a fierce, stubborn battle for the laurels. But Walcott was winning and he knew it, and Marciano was losing and he knew it. They did not know the official scoring at that point, since boxing, for no reasonable reason, never has devised a system of informing the public, the press and the fighters of the score, but Walcott led, 8-4, 7-4-1 and 7-5, on the official cards, and the fighters and their cornermen had it figured right.

"You got to knock him out," Weill screamed at Marciano as Goldman worked on Rocky's cut and bruised face.

The bell for the thirteenth round rang. Marciano tore out

of his corner and threw a left hook, which nicked Walcott's ribs. Jersey Joe backed up cautiously. Walcott cocked a right, but before he could pull the trigger, as Joe drew his hand away from his jaw and moved to his right, Marciano shot a right hand to that jaw. The punch traveled less than one foot. It was delivered with all the strength Marciano had.

It crashed against Walcott's jaw and his senses left him. His eyes closed and his knees bent and his whole body sagged as he slid down along the ropes. Marciano followed with a left which grazed Joe's head, but did not matter. Walcott sagged into a kneeling position and his hands hung limply; then his head rested loosely on the canvas and he was unconscious.

Referee Charley Daggert counted to ten and waved his hands over Walcott and turned to Marciano to raise his hand. Rocky was jumping up and down. Weill, Goldman and Colombo were coming through the ropes and rushing at him. The crowd was standing and screaming and many fans were coming out of their seats at the ring, where a wall of police checked them for a while before they broke through, knocking over typewriters in a mad rush to get at their new hero, the new champion. All was madness. And Allie Colombo hugged his boy and cried for joy.

Eventually, the announcer informed the crowd officially, "By a knockout in forty-three seconds of the thirteenth round, the winner and new champion . . . Rocky Marciano." He was cheered as few champions ever have been.

Recovered, Walcott was led away, cheered, too, by the

fans who felt he had made a great fight. He had. In the dressing room, there were tears in his eyes when he sighed and said, "I just got careless. Just for a second. Just for one second."

He'd had it and it had gotten away from him.

In Marciano's dressing room, the winner looked like a loser. His face was puffed up and bruised and caked with dried blood. His body was sweaty and sore. He smiled and said he felt "great, just great." Did he know he was behind? Yes, he thought so, he said. Was he going for the knockout? All the way, he said. Was he surprised to have been knocked down? Very surprised, he said. It never happened before. Was he surprised Walcott was so hard to knock down? He's a great fighter, Marciano said. Weill said his boy was the great fighter, and beamed, and Goldman nervously, happily fussed over him.

Later Rocky said, "Gee, but I was happy when I knew I'd won. I started to holler and jump around, and then I looked over at Jersey Joe and I began to think how bad he must feel and I couldn't dance anymore. He had fought such a great fight. I'd often wondered what it would be like to be knocked down. He showed me. It sure surprised me. But I got up, which I guess is what counts. I wonder what it's like to lose. Joe knows. I hope I never find out."

In Brockton they had been reporting Marciano's loss round by round when suddenly they announced, "Marciano is the new champion," and the startled people on the sidewalk outside the newspaper office screamed. They rushed the news to his mother, who wept with relief and joy.

In Philadelphia, Rocky kissed Barbara and was cheered for it. He was driven to a victory party, where his triumph was toasted while he sipped soft drinks and beamed. He was hurt and he was tired.

Later, he was left in his hotel room to get some rest, but he couldn't sleep. At three in the morning, he got up and dressed and walked around Rittenhouse Square and out Walnut Street and then back on Chestnut. He was surprised at how many people were up at that hour. He was a small-town boy who perhaps had never walked the streets of a big city at that hour. His coat collar was pulled up and no one recognized him.

"What could be better," he asked later, "than walking down any street in any city and knowing that you are champion?"

He went back to his room, undressed and went back to bed. Finally he fell asleep. He slept for a few hours and woke up as daylight was coming on. "I didn't know where I was, but I had a kind of feeling something good had happened," he remembered later.

Something good *had* happened.

"You know how it is," he said. "You wake up in a strange place and at first you don't know where you are. Then I remembered: Last night I won the heavyweight championship of the world."

It was hard to believe.

"When I tried to turn, my whole body was sore," he said. He got up and limped into the bathroom and looked into the mirror at the new heavyweight champion of the world.

"Over both eyes, I had cuts that had been stitched. But I was as happy as I think anybody can be."

He put white adhesive tape over the cuts. He and Barbara got dressed and went into a drugstore, took seats on stools at the counter and ordered breakfast. One writer was there and he caught Rocky's eye, and Rocky said, "Hey, come on over and pinch me."

Challenger Ezzard Charles throws a right at Rocky during their fifteen-round title bout in June, 1954. Rocky defeated the ex-champion by a unanimous decision. *United Press Photo*

8

Old Joe and Rollie Again

After winning the championship from Walcott, Marciano picked up a package at the Stadium office and got into a car for a ride to the airport and a triumphant return to Brockton. As he drove, he tossed the package up in the air and caught it. It looked like last week's laundry. "I wonder," he laughed, "what people would think if they knew this was $70,000 of Jim Norris' money?"

In this unorthodox manner, Rocky returned with his purse. Later he collected $25,000 of the theater TV money. Half went to Weill, who paid Goldman and who paid expenses. Much went to taxes. Walcott collected the lion's share, $138,000 from the gate, $50,000 from theater TV. The IBC paid more than $150,000 in federal, state and city taxes and netted $115,000. Boxing was big business.

The IBC wanted a rematch immediately. It had been a good fight with a controversial ending. Walcott had been winning until nailed by one punch. A lucky punch? Perhaps he could repeat his showing and avoid being nailed by a big punch. And the public wanted more of Marciano, the new champion. Home television and radio interests offered more than twice as much money as theater TV interests had paid for the first fight—$300,000. With home TV, the bout would have to go indoors, where it would not face the threat of a rainout.

Marciano and Weill were willing. They had a contract to fulfill and it was a logical way to go, although they were stuck with the small end of the purse. But, surprisingly, Walcott and his manager, Felix Bocchicchio, stalled. They demanded a guarantee of $250,000. After trying for weeks to talk them out of it, Norris relented on the promise of the Walcott camp that they would not reveal to Marciano's camp how much Jersey Joe was getting. The match was made for the spring in Chicago Stadium, a building owned by Norris.

Meanwhile, Marciano went home to a hero's welcome. There was a motorcade in his honor through downtown Brockton, which was not the longest ride anyone ever took. The former ditch-digger was cheered by his townspeople. Many suspected he would move now, perhaps to New York, where he could live in elegance in accordance with his newly won wealth. But Rocky never considered it. This was his home and his family's home and he was happy here.

Mayor Gerald Lucey presented Marciano with a key to the city. At a banquet, Governor Paul Dever presented him with a new Cadillac. The license plates read, "KO." Rocky still couldn't drive, at least not well. Barbara, Allie and others chauffeured him around.

At the ceremonies, Rocky's mother was asked how she felt. She said, "I cry inside. This is where my boy born, grew up, where he play. And now, look!" Her son had become the number one citizen of Brockton. And no one else had ever made the town famous.

At the time Brockton's boy won the title, Brockton was a town of 62,862 residents, many fairly recent emigrants from old countries, who worked primarily in the town's shoe factories as well as its carpet tack, storage battery and burial vault plants and sausage company. The great boxing writer W. C. Heinz did a bit of research around Brockton after Rocky made it famous and found that the town had exported more than 12 million shoes the year he won his laurels, but had produced only one champion. "Now," observed a resident, "they've heard of Brockton in places they don't even wear shoes."

When it was announced that the rematch with Walcott would be shown on home television, the Rev. Leroy Cooney, who had married Marciano and Barbara, was given a thirty-inch TV set by the new champ for the church and was so flustered while installing it that he stumbled off a stage and broke a leg.

There were somewhat nicer results. Salesmen from the town reported that when they mentioned they were from Brockton, they immediately were drawn into discussions about Marciano, and business boomed. The Howard and Foster Shoe Company, which provided Marciano with special lightweight boxing shoes, size 10-E, decided to market them. The first lot went to a men's store in Chicago. The retailer later reported the first pair was purchased by Ezzard Charles, the former heavyweight champion, who later was to challenge Marciano.

Clearly, it is a small world. But Brockton was getting bigger because of Marciano. Betting on boxing matches is illegal and an illogical way to risk hard-earned money, but it is a fact that many Brockton citizens were moved to back

the local boy heavily, and since he did not seem to know
how to lose he was, in a roundabout way, providing them
with a few luxuries they previously had been unable to
afford. Some fellows were borrowing money on or selling
their cars, betting the money on Marciano and buying better
cars.

"When Rocky fights on TV," said Bob Riordan, city editor
of Brockton's *Enterprise-Times*, "the streets are deserted.
You can look the length of Main Street and not see a soul.
Then, between rounds, you see a couple of people hurrying
across the street. They're changing bars, looking for better
reception or a better seat. The moment the fight ends, everything busts right open." When Marciano beat Walcott, all
police leaves were canceled, twenty men were assigned to
downtown and police cruisers had to rush to quell overen-
thusiastic celebrants.

The police themselves had managed to pick up a short-
wave broadcast of the nontelevised fight—but in French,
over a Canadian station. Fortunately, they had a prisoner
in from Montreal who spoke French. They had him trans-
late the reports for them. The next day, he was let off with
a light fine.

Rocky, who quit after one year of high school football,
had become a great hero in the schools. His younger brother
Peter was offered a delay of a test because it fell on the day
of the Walcott fight. He eagerly accepted. Rocky was called
on to give his old football team a pep talk at half time of a
game in which they were losing, 14–0. He so inspired them
that they rallied to win, 19–14.

Marciano retired his father from the factory to which
Rocco had carried his dad's lunch as a boy. For more than

thirty years, half his life, Perrino Marchegiano had arisen at seven every morning to run a machine that forms toes and heels of shoes. It was a difficult machine, and Perrino, still ailing from his wartime gassing, was weary of it. Gratefully, he accepted his son's offer of support.

Rocco's mother said, "It's just sit in my heart. It's hard to say the beautiful thing that happen with Rocky. You feel happy and you feel like crying when you think."

She cried with joy when, in December of 1952, Barbara presented Rocco with a daughter, Mary Anne. A father and a family man now, he bought his first house, a $35,000 nine-room ranch house at 46 Harlan Drive.

Now that Marciano was beginning to enjoy the good things of life, he had to suffer to sustain them. He went back into hard training for the second Walcott fight. He boxed 225 rounds in training. A sparring partner split his nose, which caused a month's delay from the original April date. Running roadwork, he was bitten by a dog behind the knee six days before the bout, an accident which he kept to himself for fear the fight would be called off. He said he had scratched his leg on some branches.

He had no way of knowing how much his relentless attack, powerful punches and overpowering final punch had sapped from old Jersey Joe. Rocky considered Walcott a dangerous foe, the only man who had knocked him down and the one who had come the closest to beating him, a shrewd veteran who could be expected to battle as gallantly in the second fight as he did in the first. So did the 16,034 fans who paid up to forty dollars to see the bout on the night of May 15. Millions gathered expectantly before their TV sets and around their radios.

The bell rang and the two fighters moved out at each other. At first, they fought cautiously. At the one-minute mark, Marciano began to open up. He missed some blows which may have made Walcott nervous and landed some which made Walcott hurt. Jersey Joe moved around in his dancing shuffle, warily. Just past the two-minute mark, Marciano hit Walcott with a left-right combination to the head. Jersey Joe settled into a sitting position on the canvas with his right arm hooked over the ropes. He sat there as referee Frank Sikora counted over him and fans screamed at him to rise. At the count of nine, Walcott shifted. At ten, he sprang up. By then, Sikora was waving his arms in front of Joe, indicating the count was completed, the bout suddenly over. Two minutes and 25 seconds had elapsed.

Walcott turned and started toward his corner. The crowd hooted. Walcott turned back and began to argue with Sikora, making angry gestures, saying that he had been victimized by a "fast count." But it was too late.

Joe was asked, "You wouldn't want to try it again, would you?" He didn't answer.

In the dressing room, he praised Marciano as an overpowering puncher and said that he had been badly hurt but had gotten confused in the count and had been prepared to carry on and perhaps launch a rally.

He never fought again. He took his final $250,000 and retired from the ring. Marciano collected $166,038. Neither was bad pay for less than three minutes' work. But it left many with an empty feeling after eight months of debate and buildup.

Pleased as he was with the knockout and the money, Marciano was displeased by the unsatisfactory conclusion.

As a champion now, he wanted the opportunity to make a more impressive showing. And as champion now, he could get the big end of a purse. But it had to be an attractive bout.

The logical foe was Roland LaStarza, who never had been given a rematch with Marciano or a title shot by Charles or Walcott. Many felt LaStarza had deserved the decision in the first Walcott fight, and had proven he could handle Marciano.

LaStarza was big, strong and tough, a good hitter and a better boxer. Also he was young. And he was unafraid of Marciano, since he was one who felt he had beaten him the first time around. The match was made fast, for the Polo Grounds in New York in September. Weill took 42.5 percent for Marciano. LaStarza's camp settled for 17.5 percent. They wanted the chance at the champ as Marciano had wanted the chance at Walcott.

The fight drew a great crowd of almost 45,000 fans. With TV and radio money, Marciano made a score of almost $200,000, while LaStarza took in more than $70,000. They earned every penny. In contrast to the second Walcott fight, this one was hard work.

Goldman feared LaStarza, with justification. Rollie was a classy fighter. He stood up straight and jabbed fast and hard. He could keep Rocky off with a jab while crossing and counterpunching him with a strong right cross.

Goldman figured out perhaps the most unorthodox plan of attack ever devised for a heavyweight champion. He warned Marciano that he would have as much trouble piercing LaStarza's defenses as he had Walcott's in the first fight with Jersey Joe. He warned Marciano that LaStarza

would jab him almost as effectively as Louis had. LaStarza
was younger and stronger than Walcott and Louis had been.
But Goldman understood better than anyone the awesome
power of Marciano's punches. "Hit him on the arms," Goldman instructed Marciano. "The arms will start hurting before the rest of him and he won't be able to keep them up."

Before the first Walcott fight, Goldman had told Marciano
that sometimes when Joe prepared to throw a right hand,
he moved to his right. Several times during that fight,
Marciano thought of this, but he either did not catch it in
time or was unable to use it. In the thirteenth round he
thought of it, and when Walcott started to throw his right,
he shifted to his right and Marciano used it, lunging in with
the short, straight punch that ruined old Jersey Joe. Respect-
ing Goldman's advice, Rocky accepted his curious strategy.

It was not easy. He was a headhunter, who bore in swinging for home runs. Body-punching was a part of the business
and he could see the sense of pounding at a foe's midsection
in close—but hit him on the arms? From the first bell, with
the crowd urging him on, Marciano swung for the head and
pounded at the body and whenever he did not see good
openings he simply punched LaStarza's arms.

LaStarza kept pumping that jab in Rocky's face, like a
piston, and crossing with the right. Marciano kept boring
in, relentlessly, punching heavily. In the sixth, he was pe-
nalized for low blows and lost the round. In the seventh,
he was cut and began to bleed, and in missing a punch at
one point he stumbled clumsily and went down awkwardly,
embarrassed. Still, he kept coming on and on.

Marciano's gloved fists broke blood vessels and bones in

LaStarza's arms and elbows. First the arms grew heavy, then they began to ache awfully, then they grew numb. As the relentless battle wore on, LaStarza found it harder and harder to raise his arms, much less jab with them or punch with them. His hands lowered, his defense dissipated. Marciano began to punish him about the head. LaStarza began to take a terrible beating. Still, he fought on gamely.

In the eleventh round, Marciano drove a left hook and a right cross to LaStarza's head with devastating force. The brutal blows stunned the gallant youngster, who was driven down into the ropes. Desperately, he tried to rise, but then he sagged back, helpless. He simply could not move. He was beaten and it was over.

Three years of bitter controversy had been resolved. The crowd roared a tribute to the champion, who had proven himself.

In his dressing room, a badly battered LaStarza, his face swollen and broken, his arms hanging helplessly at his sides, mumbled, "He was just too much for me."

A bruised and weary Marciano sighed, "He could take more punishment . . ." His words drifted off. Himself a fighter who never stopped, he seemed awed by LaStarza's reluctance to quit.

If ever he doubted the brutality of this business, this showing by his foe seemed to convince him even more than his own showing against Walcott. "Sometimes it's easier to take punishment than to punish someone," he said. "You're always afraid of hurting someone," he said, perhaps thinking of Carmine Vingo. "But you can't help hurting people in the ring," he sighed.

"Sometimes," he said, "it is not a very easy business."

Defending heavyweight champ bores into Don Cockell, British challenger. Marciano won by a TKO in the ninth round, May, 1955. *United Press Photo*

9

The Champion

Once, while doing roadwork near a public golf course, Rocky Marciano idly stopped to pick up a stray golf ball from the street. An angry golfer rushed up to him, brandishing his club and threatening to slug him if he didn't return the ball. Clearly, he did not recognize the heavyweight champion of the world. Nor was it in Rocky's nature to strut his stature. Amused, he smiled and handed the ball over, and the golfer stormed off.

Not everyone recognized Rocky. At a dinner, he was introduced to an elderly gentleman. "What did you say your name is?" the gentleman asked. He had come to understand that this was an athlete, but he didn't catch the name. Marciano repeated his name politely. The old man shrugged. "I don't follow baseball much," he said.

However, most persons did recognize Marciano wherever he went. This was another era in boxing, a boom period for the sport, when television brought the leading fighters into homes as well as theaters across the country, and Rocky Marciano, the Brockton Blockbuster, the colorful and explosive heavyweight champion of the world, was the single most prominent athlete around, better known than Stan Musial, Otto Graham, George Mikan, Ben Hogan or the other great stars of sports of the early 1950's.

Those heavyweight champions who have followed Marciano—Floyd Patterson, Sonny Liston, Cassius Clay, Joe Frazier and the rest—have never achieved anything near the popularity of Marciano. Possibly his popularity was due in part to an unfortunate reason. He was the first white heavyweight champion in fifteen years and the last and only one in fifteen more years since, except for the brief, one-year reign of Sweden's Ingemar Johansson.

However, we prefer to believe that Rocky's unusual popularity was due more to his incredible record and his appealing personality.

He was the first undefeated boxer to attain the heavyweight title, he always fought gallantly and he knocked out most of his opponents. His very gracelessness may have been an asset, since it caused the ordinary persons who watched and envied him to imagine themselves somehow being determined enough and powerful enough to do what he did. He was not a trapeze artist or ballet dancer, whose accomplishments seem beyond us.

Yet he wore his laurels with striking modesty. He was no handsome Greek god, but a short, stocky, homely person who might have been your next-door neighbor. He had a high-pitched voice and spoke with a broad New England accent which sounded strange coming out of that boxer's mug. He never swore. He was polite and friendly to all who met him and was never heard to say a bad word about anyone. He did not try to rise above reporters as do some athletes who attain prominence. He even welcomed some into his hotel suite and spoke with them freely only hours before the second Walcott fight, at a time when most fighters would be irritable and in seclusion. He obviously did not enjoy hurting people in the ring. It was his profession, the only way he had found to make life better for himself and for his family.

He adored his wife and daughter, and it distressed him deeply when training and the demands of public appearances kept him apart from them.

Once, on the road, he saw a picture of his daughter in the papers and thought her eyes looked strange. When he got home, he saw that she had a slight cross-eyed condition and asked his wife about it. She said others had noticed it. "Why didn't you mention it?" he asked. "When do you have time to listen?" she said. He never forgot this. Fortunately, the eye condition was corrected.

In the only instance in which he challenged Weill's authority, Marciano insisted his wife be permitted to stay with him in a small cottage at his training camp during his long pre-fight preparations.

"I think my schedule is hardest on my wife. She is left alone a lot of the time. But she seldom complains. She shoulders twice her share of the burden and she accepts our life as it is," Rocky sighed.

The life he led was hard on his parents, too. They wanted theirs to be a close family, as Rocky did. But he simply did not have the time.

Once, his mother said, "Rocco, there's something I would like to talk with you about."

He said, "Sure, Mom, anytime you want."

She said, "You are so important now I don't like to bother you."

He was hurt by this and said, "Please, Mom. You can never bother me. I'm your son."

She sighed and said, "I've been thinking that there is so much pleasure you're missing. When your sister has a baby and when somebody gets married, it is a beautiful thing, but you are so busy you can't be there."

He said, "I know, Mom." He felt bad about it.

Once he mused, "I didn't see my sister Concetta's baby until it was six months old. When my friend Nicky Sylvester got married, I couldn't go to the wedding. But I only get to see my own wife and baby about four months out of every year."

When he was home, it was no longer as it had been before. "When I get together with my old friends in Brockton, it isn't the same," he admitted. "I never do find out how they feel and what they're thinking, and we never have the laughs about the little things we used to have before. They seem to be uncomfortable with me, like I'm no longer one of them, and I don't know how to let them know I still want to be. They drop in and they leave fast. They're afraid they're bothering me."

His wife said much the same thing. "I enjoy being with the girls and we're fine when there's just us, but when the talk turns to Rocky or when Rocky's around, it's as though he was in another world from them and it makes them uncomfortable, as though they didn't belong. It spoils things and it stops being easy between me and my friends. I guess life just can't ever again be the way it was."

It could not be. He was now the champion of the world. He was advised not even to be in Brockton during a layoff because it came at a time during a close battle for the mayor's position; and Rocky, who did not want to get involved in politics, was cautioned that if he showed any preference he might swing the election. Rocky and Barbara killed the long time in New York.

Another year, another election, a leading candidate came to Rocky's house and asked if he could meet him, shake hands with him and speak to him for just a few minutes because no one could believe a prominent politician in Brockton did not know Marciano, and he wanted to be able to tell them he did, indeed, know him, with some degree of honesty. Rocky made him feel at home.

When he bought his new home, a neighbor counted five hundred cars which drove by and paused to look at it the first weekend. There were always people around that place, looking in the windows, knocking on the door and asking for autographs. Late one night he returned unexpectedly from a trip and there were no strangers around. Allie Colombo recalled taking a walk with Rocky the next morning and Rocky saying, "You know, it was great to come back to my own home and to wake up and find my wife and the baby there and to have nobody else around."

"We walked about five or six miles," Allie recalled, "and when we got back, there they were—five cars in front of the house."

Rocky averaged a hundred letters a day, some of them from distant, exotic lands, most asking for autographs or pictures or souvenirs or pieces of equipment, such as shoes and gloves, which might be used for charity raffles. Much of the mail was turned over to an old friend of Rocky's, Arthur Bellao, and his wife, who had a typewriter and volunteered to help with the mail when Rocky first began to become famous, but soon found themselves working eight hours a day to take care of it.

One of the mailmen who delivered the Brockton mail was Red Gormley, who returned from North Carolina with Rocky as baseball failures in 1947 and was offered the chance to manage Marciano's planned ring career, but did nothing about it. Now he carried letters to the home of Rocky's family. "So what's the sense of talking about it?" he said. "I've got a wife and three kids now." And letters to deliver.

The doctor who delivered him, Dr. Josephat Phaneuf, who delivered more than 7,000 babies in Brockton, admitted he might be one of the few persons in Brockton who never claimed to have seen him fight. "A great many of my patients talk about him, though," said the doctor, "and when they do, I say I was the first one ever to hit him."

Their son's celebrity in town made the Marchegianos faintly uncomfortable. The mother said, "I was on the street and a woman come up to me. She say, 'God bless you, Mrs. Marchegiano. My son and my son-in-law they make a fortune on your boy. I tell no one, but I tell you because I want to thank you.'" Mrs. Marchegiano shook her head with wonder. "Who is this woman?" she asked.

"I don't go downtown. Too much talk," the father said. He visited the factory where he worked so long and his old friends said, "What a difference, Pete. Years ago you couldn't talk with the super, and now he wants to take you around the shop."

Being a celebrity and a champion had other disadvantages. Rocky was subjected to some hate mail, including some frightening letters. After he knocked out Louis, he got a letter saying if he came to Brockton for the celebration he'd be shot. Police were able to trace the letter and discovered it had been written by a thirteen-year-old girl. Still, such letters made Rocky uneasy. Before his next fight, against Ezzard Charles, he got a letter saying if he beat Charles he'd be killed because Charles was a gentleman and he, Marciano, was a bully. Rocky had friends stay with his family during and after the fight. "I never imagined I'd put my family through anything like this," he sighed.

Once, he said, "You end up a lonesome guy in a crowd." He said being a champion and a celebrity wore on him sometimes. "It's a full-time job," he sighed, "and the influence you have on people is sometimes so strong that it worries you and can even bring tears to your eyes." People looked up to him because he had become a champion and was making money in sums they never dreamed of making, and some were dependent on him for their living, and many demanded his friendship and asked his advice.

Basically, he was a simple man of simple tastes. Trying champagne at a victory party, he almost gagged and embarrassedly had to switch to his customary Coke. He did not smoke. He liked movies and Broadway shows; his idea of really good shows was "Guys and Dolls" and "Stalag 17." He read sports stories and "whodunits."

He was religious and wore St. Anthony and St. Rocco medals, which he carried into the ring in the pockets of his robe, not being permitted to wear them in the ring. He was surprised when he was asked to speak for the priests and nuns at St. Colman's Parish. He was always ready to speak to youth groups. He liked money, but never asked for fees.

Once, the Prince of Siam was a guest at Grossinger's, where Rocky was training. The phone rang in Rocky's quarters and he was asked if he would permit the prince to visit him before he left. Rocky rushed around getting ready like a teen-age girl about to receive a movie star. "I was just lying around in a T-shirt, watching TV. I hadn't shaved or anything," he recalled later. Swiftly, he showered and shaved, changed into clean, neat clothes, then sat around and waited for the visitor who never came. "I guess he got busy," Rocky said, disappointed, but not offended. As it was, the prince's group had decided he did not have time to visit Marciano before he had to leave for the airport.

Rocky spoke with awe of having met President Eisenhower, Ty Cobb, Cy Young, Ben Hogan and others at a Sports Luncheon at the Waldorf-Astoria Hotel. "So you're the heavyweight champion of the world," Ike said.

"Yes, sir," Rocky said.

Ike stepped back and studied the squat Marciano. "You know," the President said, "somehow I thought you'd be bigger."

"No, sir," Rocky said.

Rocky went on several exhibition tours in which he was hailed as a conquering hero. On one tour of Maine, his brother Louis boxed him several rounds under an assumed name. Rocky figured Louis might as well get the work as anyone, and it really didn't matter whom he sparred with. But Louis was no pro, and it was all illegal, and Rocky was suspended for thirty days. It didn't matter because he had no bouts scheduled in that period, anyway. But it always bothered Rocky, since it was the only smear of any sort on his record.

Rocky, Weill, Goldman and sparring partners Bob Golden and Toxie Hall made a five-week, 30,000-mile exhibition tour of the Pacific area after Marciano won the title. In Manila, mobs waited for him wherever he went. Once, Rocky was walking down the street when a fellow driving by suddenly stopped his car, jumped out, ran over and shook Rocky's hand, then ran back to the car, jumped in and drove off.

Asked to box on Sunday, Rocky declined. "I'm a Roman Catholic and I go to church on Sunday," he said. But he boxed every other day for more than a month, luring great, responsive crowds.

He was making a lot of money, but he never could forget being poor, and to say he was close with a dollar probably is understating the case. Al Weill recalled, "The first time Rocky earned a good purse, it was like feeding a bowl of blood to a tiger." The more Rocky made, the less it seemed to him. In 1953, for example, he pointed out that, after taxes, "I came out with a lot less than $100,000." Wistfully, he commented, "When I fight twice a year, I don't get to keep more than $15,000 out of the second fight"—which, with the ascending scale of taxes, was the reason he did not fight three or four times a year.

He often reminisced about the $1,200 he had won on a troopship during the war, most of which he loaned out and little of which he ever got back. It taught him a lesson. "I don't know whatever happened to that money, but it wasn't put to good use," he sighed.

He was bothered by the people who wanted to spend his money for him. "They run at you with all kinds of business schemes," he pointed out. "There are people who want me to sign notes for them or loan them money or sponsor them in their careers. They've tried to sell me uranium and copper mines and oil wells and a dairy."

He was disturbed by some tearful pleas for money which he got in the mail. Once he said, "I got a letter from a woman I don't even know but she wrote that if I'd give her $1,500, her little boy could be made well again."

"How do you think I feel?" he asked.

Rocky's father said his son always hated to spend money. He recalled, "Mama used to give him a quarter sometimes to go to the movies. Like on Saturday afternoon. He would put it in his pocket and go out. That night, after he got in bed, she would be hanging up his clothes and the quarter would fall out. He didn't spend it." The old man shook his head affectionately. "He always hated to spend money, that boy. He was always working for a dollar. His pleasure was giving money to Mama."

One of Rocky's dreams was to send his parents back to Italy for a visit. He went for the cost, but he was deeply disappointed when it did not work out as he hoped it would. First, he was too busy to see them off at the airport. Then he was surprised to have them return much earlier than planned. They had gone to his father's hometown and returned to the United States without even going to his mother's hometown. "Too much sadness there," they said. "Every place we went, they had nothing, and they looked to us and how much we could do."

Another dream of his was to give a giant party for every boy and girl in Brockton after he won the title. He never did it.

Once, Rocky refereed a wrestling match for Baltimore promoter Benny Trotta. On the drive back to the airport, Rocky suddenly said, "Stop, I have to make a phone call."

"Why?" Trotta asked.

"I got to call the arena," Rocky said. "I left my sweat socks there and they're brand new."

"That's ridiculous," Trotta said.

"I just paid two dollars for them," Rocky said.

Concluded Trotta, "He'll never die broke."

Al Weill, a free spender, told of a time he had taken a two-day business trip with Rocky and found him brushing his teeth with his finger.

"I left my toothbrush at home," Marciano explained.

"Ain't they got drugstores in this town?" asked Weill.

On another occasion, Weill reported that Marciano left home for a three-day trip with three dollars in his pocket, figuring this would cover his miscellaneous expenses.

"He gave autographs in place of tips," Weill said.

On the other hand, Rocky was generous with family and

friends. Toots Shor, the noted restaurateur and friend of athletes, recalled, "I'll never forget when I had my joint closed for more than a year. One night Marciano comes over to see me and he's clutching $5,000 in a big fist, and in that choirboy voice of his, he says, "This is all I can spare right now, Toots, but maybe it'll come in handy as walking-around money." Sighed Toots, "How about that! A guy hears your crummy saloon is closed and he figures you're in a jam and he volunteers to help you. Well, that was Rocky Marciano."

The Rock never was comfortable with money or position, though he handled himself with class. He wanted to feel he had brought happiness to some people close to him. He was so proud his dad was proud of him, he disregarded the fact that the old man, too, was uncomfortable with money and fame, and was pleased that he could be a prominent part of his training camps.

Years later Rocky said, "My father was always a great one for making me proud. He was a sickly man who never made better than seventy-five dollars a week in his life, and when I started fighting, it was like a whole new world opened up for him. He became a big man in Brockton. In the training camp he did a lot of little things for me and he felt important. He was a great help."

Rocky never permitted an entourage of hangers-on and free-loaders to gather around him as they gathered around other great champions such as Joe Louis, Sugar Ray Robinson and Willie Pep, but he always included his father in the group. He also included Allie Colombo and sometimes other friends, but he was always aware the grand ride would end sometime. Once at camp he said, "Someday, this ship's gonna reach port, gang, and that's as far as we go together." Then he hugged his father and said, "Not you, Pop."

Archie Moore stands over Marciano in second round.
Rocky KO'd Moore in the ninth round.   *United*
Press Photo

10

Ezz

If being the heavyweight champion and earning a lot of money and gaining prominence were not without their problems, Rocky Marciano rarely complained about such things because he was well aware how much better off he was than most people. "How can I complain?" he once said. It's just that he was basically a simple person who was not at home in the spotlight under pressure.

One of the hardest things about being a top athlete and especially a top fighter was the heavy training that was necessary to stay on top. Few athletes ever were so naturally gifted they could attain and hold a position at the top without constant training, and many have partied their way out of prominence.

Marciano never was much for parties, and he required heavier conditioning periods than most fighters because he was not a stylist, but depended on strength and stamina to overpower his foes. Many of his fights were finished fast, but he never knew when he might have to go 10 or 11 hard rounds to beat a Roland LaStarza or 13 hard rounds to beat a Joe Walcott, or more, though no one yet had gone 15 rounds with him.

And 15 rounds is a longer, harder route than it seems. That's 45 minutes of fighting, an hour in the ring with one-minute rest periods between rounds. Just try holding your arms up for 45 minutes in 15 three-minute sections, much less punching with them and being punched on them.

When a fighter is in the round, he is not a baseball player standing around between pitches or a football player walking back into position between plays or a basketball player standing around during free throws, but a man who, even if it is not a fast-fought fight, must be on the alert at all times. One mistake and he will not give up a home run or a touchdown or a basket, but may be knocked out. And if it is a fast-fought fight, and goes a distance, it can be extremely grueling.

Unlike many other fighters, Marciano never minded training, apart from the time it took him away from his family. From the time he began to box, he never was out of training. He prepared for most of his big bouts at Grossinger's in the Catskill Mountains, and after he won the title he was up there far more than he was away.

Even when he had no match coming up, he would live like a monk in his cottage at Grossinger's Airport, doing roadwork in the morning, hitting the bags or boxing with sparring partners in the gym, which was a converted hangar, in the afternoon and taking hikes at night.

When he had a big fight, he would spend eight to twelve weeks in camp. At his insistence, his wife and child would spend the first part of the time with him, but when it got serious, she would leave.

The last ten days or so, he would not be permitted to take telephone calls or read newspapers or even watch too much television. Weill and Goldman mothered him as though he was an infant, fearful of his being exposed to anything that might break his concentration or disturb him.

"They were even careful about what we'd talk about," Rocky once said wistfully.

Weill was the absolute boss because this was his nature, and Marciano was willing to accept this. Al liked the spotlight and didn't like to share it even with his champion.

"You gotta take orders, you know," the Rock shrugged.

Rocky was sorry when he was shut off from writers, but Weill was reluctant to permit too many interviews. Once he told a writer, "You, Mr. Gordon, don't you try that interviewing Rocky alone. You interview me. I'm 'the Vest,' and I get all the gravy."

"Mr. Gordon" was David Condon, the fine *Chicago Tribune* journalist.

So the training went on. Rocky was proud of his body. He understood the pain it would have to bear. Sometimes he would run an extra mile or train an extra few rounds because if it enabled him to go one more minute of the fight at top speed it would be worth it. Wearing protective headgear, he worked hard with his sparring partners because he felt if he loafed he would develop bad habits which might follow him into the real fights.

In between, he prowled restlessly around the camp and

his cottage, cut off from the world, frequently lonely, after his wife left. Yet he was unwilling to go to the big hotel down the road where top entertainers were performing for carefree vacationers for fear it would make him soft or relaxed. He would lie on a couch, sprawl in a chair, pace around half-watching television, waiting, waiting, waiting.

Because he was proud of his body, he became something of a health-food addict, but the hardest part of training for him was staying away from the foods he loved. He was an incredible eater with a great taste for calorie-rich Italian dishes. One time his mother made a roast chicken and put it in the refrigerator for some guests she had coming to the house. When she went to get it, it was gone. She asked Rocky about it. He told the truth, red-faced. He had eaten the entire chicken. He had been hungry.

Once a friend of Rocky's, Jimmy Careglia, whom Rocky made known as "Jimmy Tomatoes" because he made a lot of money growing tomatoes, gave a party for Rocky. The champion ate a big bowl of minestrone soup, a large helping of lasagna (noodles, meat and cheese), a five-pound sirloin steak, two filet mignons and a big bowl of ice cream. This was a typical dinner. A typical breakfast was a bowl of cold cereal with a raw egg in it, two soft-boiled eggs, two lamb chops, two slices of toast, two baked apples and a cup of hot tea.

After a Red Sox game one night, Ted Williams invited Rocky to his apartment to eat. When they settled down, Williams set down a quart of ice cream for each of them. Rocky thought this was odd, eating dessert first, but he went along with his host and politely demolished his quart. Williams went out and came back with two more quarts. "What's this?" Rocky asked. "When do we eat?" Ted explained he never ate anything but ice cream after a game. Marciano was stunned. Politely he ate more and more ice cream along with his host. Finally, Rocky escaped. He rushed to a restaurant for steak and spaghetti. He seldom ate ice cream after that.

Rocky always insisted his appetite was ordinary. He was impressed with how much the tiny Goldman could put away, for example. But Goldman always claimed he was just trying to keep the food away from Marciano. Once, Goldman ate three big plates of spaghetti in a row. When Rocky sat down, the serving bowl was almost empty. "Hey," he complained, "there's nothing left for me."

"That," Goldman smiled, "was the idea."

Goldman always suspected Marciano was sneaking food on the side and kept on the alert lest Rocky eat himself out of condition. One night before the first Walcott fight, Rocky got up from in front of the TV set, stretched and said loudly, "Well, I guess I'll hit the sack."

It still was early and Rocky had had a long nap that afternoon. The wheels clicked in Goldman's head and he instantly was suspicious. "What'd you stash in your room tonight?" he asked. "You been buying some salami or something?"

Rocky was insulted. "What's the matter, Charlie, aren't you ever gonna start trusting me?" he asked sadly.

Goldman muttered something and Rocky shook his head

unhappily and went to his room—where, as he later happily admitted, he took a two-pound salami from under his pillow and began to attack it.

Still, he limited his excesses and always stayed hard at 184. He forced himself to pass up the starches as the big fights drew near. He ran and punched the big bag until he was exhausted. He sweated in the gym until Goldman and Weill had to chase him away. Possibly no athlete ever trained harder. "Rocky," Frank Graham said, "is addicted to exercise as some men are addicted to the bottle."

"I like training," Rocky once said. "I like working up for a big fight and the way people treat you afterward."

He did not pretend he was a stylist. "My long suit is determination," he said. "It becomes a kind of religion. You believe in yourself and you believe in the things you got to do and you never forget them for a minute.

"I don't like hitting or being hit, but it's a business," he said. "I never think about getting hurt. I can handle fear. I put it out of sight. If you don't prepare properly, it pops in front of you and you're finished. If you do prepare properly, you have control,"

He was modest about his victories. Before the second fight with LaStarza, he was asked about the first fight. "Oh, it was an *ah*ful good fight," he said in his flat New England accent. "I thought I won it, but I guess some didn't. It was an *ah*ful good fight." He sounded like a fan.

"What it comes down to in the ring," he once explained, "is that it's the other guy or you. Anybody in there with me is there to get me and I'm in there to get him, but the one thing people don't seem to understand is that there's nothing personal about it."

He had become confident about his ability. "I don't think anybody in the world can lick me," he said. Yet he was a realist. He smiled. "Sometimes I think, suppose the other guy thinks like me?" he said. "What will happen to my plans then?"

One who thought he could beat him and had a chance was Ezzard Charles, perhaps, all things considered, the best fighter Marciano ever fought. Louis, Walcott and later Archie Moore were still outstanding but aging when Rocky met them. LaStarza was clever and Layne powerful, but neither compared to Charles. Ezzard may have been the most underrated heavyweight champion of all time.

After winning a series of top amateur championships as a middleweight, Charles turned pro in 1940 and became a tremendous light-heavyweight. A brilliant boxer and powerful puncher, he won 20 straight fights, 14 by knockout, before he lost his first fight, to former middleweight champion Ken Overlin.

Ezz never got a shot at the light-heavyweight title, but he beat some great fighters as he went on, decisioning onetime light-heavy king Joey Maxim three times, Jimmy Bivins twice and Charley Burley twice, knocking out former light-heavyweight champion Anton Christoforidis, decisioning Archie Moore twice and knocking him out once.

He had been fighting ten years, ducked by champions but never ducking anyone, losing only four times, each to an outstanding fighter, when he got his chance at the heavyweight title vacated by Louis in 1949. He outpointed Maxim in an elimination bout, then outpointed Walcott in a championship fight.

Charles was a rare fighting champion, defending his title nine times in two years and one month, beating Walcott in a rematch, beating Maxim in a rematch, beating Louis, who came out of retirement, knocking out light-heavyweight champion Gus Lesnevich, Pat Valentino, Freddie Beshore, Nick Barone and Lee Oma, before giving Walcott another chance. This was Walcott's fifth title shot (two against Louis and three against Charles), and he was behind when he caught Ezzard with a perfect punch and knocked him out.

Walcott honored his contract for a rematch and gained a highly questionable decision over Charles and never gave him another chance. Ezzard continued to campaign, losing a few to good fighters, beating some good fighters, before Marciano's camp booked him for a championship match on June 15, 1954, in Yankee Stadium, New York. After two nights of postponements, it came off on the seventeenth.

Charles was almost thirty-three years old and had fought more than a hundred professional fights over fifteen years when he met Marciano, but the fresh opportunity revived most of his old ambition and skill. He trained hard and was sharp by the night of the fight.

While Marciano was a 7–2 favorite, many writers and fans respected Charles's brilliance and conceded him a chance of outmaneuvering and perhaps cutting up the bull-like champion. A crowd of nearly 50,000 persons paid more than half-a-million dollars to see the bout, while theater-television operators paid $350,000 more to beam it across the country.

Few spectacles are as dramatic as a heavyweight championship bout in a big ballpark under the stars. The cheapest seats in the distant pews go for $5 or $10. Ringside seats, which may stretch as far as the eye can see, go for $30 or $40, as in this case, or $50 or, on occasion, $100. The big spenders strut down the aisles to their select locations. Movie and TV stars and celebrities of other sports fill the select spots.

The great crowd gathers and the tension thickens and at 10:00 or 10:30, the great fighters present are introduced in the ring—perhaps a Sugar Ray Robinson, resplendent in outrageous finery, which draws a roar from the crowd, or perhaps a Joe Louis, who always gets the most applause.

The fighters in their robes and hoods dance down the aisles as their handlers and police clear a path for them, and the noise of the crowd rises as they spring into the ring and bounce around, loosening up.

They are introduced and given their instructions. "You stand in your corner trying to concentrate and look up at that tremendous crowd surrounding you in all those tremendous tiers in a place like Yankee Stadium and it sends a shiver through you," Marciano once confessed.

The ballpark lights dim, the floodlights pour onto the ring, which suddenly seems small, the bell rings and the two fighters move out at one another. There is a constant electricity of excitement generated by the crowd, which is alert for that one punch which may suddenly end it all. With every big punch, every rally, the crowd comes up roaring and the noise is like thunder.

For four rounds, Rocky couldn't find the coffee-colored Charles. Ezz was there, but like a will-o'-the-wisp, boxing beautifully, hooking with his left hand to the body, countering with right crosses to the head, slipping Marciano's fearful blows. Late in the fourth round, Charles moved in on Marciano and whipped away with both hands to Rocky's body, then suddenly stepped back and delivered a combination to Marciano's head which cut Rocky over the left eye.

This was a fight, the crowd could see that, and the fans were screaming. Rocky began to rally in the fifth, bleeding and more determined than ever, coming on hard and reaching Charles with heavy punches to the head. He hit Ezzard with a strong left hook on the jaw, but Ezzard took it well and returned his own left hook to the jaw which hurt Marciano at the bell.

Through the sixth and seventh, they battled furiously, exchanging good punches. But Charles stood up and fought. He was getting hurt, but he accepted it and he continued to outbox Marciano, and hurt him on occasion, too. In the eighth and ninth, Charles gave as much as he took. In the tenth, however, he was staggered by stormy right hands several times.

They were in the last third now and everyone was excited by the tense struggle. Most suspected Charles was ahead in points, but the tide seemed to be turning in Marciano's favor. Both were tired, but battling on. In the eleventh, twelfth and thirteenth rounds, Charles would outbox Marciano only to be caught by a left hook or overhand right or short chopping right, which would jar him and cause his knees to quiver.

Still, he carried on, bruised and terribly tired, taking

heavy punishment, but fighting back with good combinations. Marciano had to fight farther than any other time in his career. He had to go through a fifteenth round, not certain he had pulled ahead in points, trying desperately to land a knockdown or knockout punch, but he could not.

When the final bell rang, the crowd gave the two sore and weary fighters a standing ovation that lasted a full minute. Then they awaited the decision. The fighters and their crews waited.

Johnny Addie picked up the scorecards and took the microphones as the crowd hushed. He read the result: "Judge Harold Barnes: eight rounds for Marciano, six rounds for Charles, one even. Referee Ruby Goldstein: eight rounds for Marciano, five rounds for Charles, two even. Judge Artie Aidala: nine rounds Marciano, five rounds Charles, one even. The winner and still heavyweight champion of the world—Ro-cky Mar-ci-ano!"

And the crowd screamed for him and cheered his gallant victim as they left the ring. In his dressing room, a dreadfully disappointed Charles said, "I thought I won. I thought I won. I really thought I won." His face was bruised and swollen. He was so tired his voice was soft and weak. "He throws a lot of punches," Ezz sighed. "He's awfully strong."

In Marciano's room, the cut and battered champion admitted, "It was my toughest fight, much tougher than the first Walcott fight. Walcott outboxed me, but I knocked him out in the end. Charles not only outboxed me, but he mixed with me, and I couldn't knock him out. I couldn't even knock him down."

There was a great demand for another fight between the two and it was arranged swiftly, for just three months later, mid-September, back in Yankee Stadium. The two immediately went back into heavy training as soon as the wounds of their first meeting had healed. The buildup began anew.

Television interests were so eager for the fight that the IBC decided to split it among several. Home TV and radio interests paid $135,000 for some areas, while theater TV grossed more than $500,000 in other areas. All this cut sharply into the live gate, but almost 35,000 fans paid more than $350,000 to see the rematch, which was again twice postponed by rain to September 17.

Most wanted to see for themselves, but few felt Charles could stand up to Marciano's murderous attack a second time. Many remembered Walcott's pathetic showing in his second time around with Marciano. But Charles was something special, a brilliant and brave performer.

He was floored by a long right hand in the second round, but he got up to fight better than ever. He moved around Marciano, outboxing him, and when drawn into an exchange, punched with him. And in the sixth round he turned loose a barrage of punches which split Marciano's nose vertically and badly.

Early in his career, Marciano had experienced trouble with his nose. Before the second Walcott fight, which was in Chicago during the winter, Marciano trained in cold weather in Holland, Michigan. Despite the cold, he slept with the windows wide open. He began to suffer from a runny nose. In training, sparring partners hit him on the nose and it began to bleed. A doctor diagnosed a ruptured blood vessel and the bout had to be postponed a month.

Walcott never got a chance to hurt the nose in that bout, nor had LaStarza or Charles in the first bout managed to damage it heavily; but now in the second bout Charles had laid it open like a cantaloupe that had been cleaved with a butcher knife, and Ezzard targeted it with swift, devastating punches. The crowd screamed at the sight of the 4–1 underdog on the verge of a great upset.

Between rounds, the doctor rushed into the ring to examine the wound, which was awful, but he was not yet ready to stop the fight, reluctant to deprive a man of his championship because of an injury which might do him no permanent harm. Weill screamed at Marciano to go for a knockout. In the seventh, Marciano went for it more determinedly than ever.

He attacked with a force that was frightening, pouring into Charles and clubbing the challenger with tremendous punches. Charles's body seemed to shudder under the impact of these wallops. He counterattacked as well as he could, battering and bloodying Marciano's nose further, but Ezz was punished heavily, though he did not go down.

Between the seventh and eighth rounds, Weill seemed to be wrestling with the doctor as he impeded his progress into the ring to reexamine the wound. The doctor decided to let Marciano go one more round. It was all he needed.

He charged Charles. For nearly two minutes he battered him. A long right hand knocked Ezzard down. Badly hurt, but trying hard, Charles got up. He tried to hold on. Marciano shrugged him off. He hooked the left to Ezzard's chin and clubbed a right to the side of Ezzard's head, and the challenger's eyes went vacant and he collapsed.

Charles was counted out with twenty-six seconds remaining in the round.

Recovered, Charles was led to his dressing room. At an interview, there were tears in his eyes. "After I cut his nose and his eye, I thought I was going to win. I didn't think he could go more than two or three more rounds," he said. He shook his head wistfully. "Maybe he couldn't have. He didn't have to. You'll have to tell me what hit me in the eighth. It seemed like everything did."

Patched up, Marciano answered questions in his quarters. "My nose feels pretty bad, but I won, so I feel pretty good," he said. "Yes, I was afraid they'd stop it. I don't know if they would have, but I finished him before they did. He's a good fighter, I want to tell you."

But he was not good enough to beat Marciano. No one who had fought him was.

After he recovered, Charles continued in the ring, on and off, for five years, reluctant to retire, but he had little left and he demeaned his record with losses late in his long career. Finally he retired and prospered for a while, but then he was crippled with disease and confined to a wheelchair.

Marciano, himself, continued on for a while. He collected more than $200,000 from the first Charles fight and more than $250,000 from the second. In three months, he had earned nearly half-a-million dollars. But he had paid a heavy price for it. His face had been mauled severely. More important, his private life had been affected.

Just prior to the first Charles fight, Rocky's pregnant wife had suffered a miscarriage. Rather than worry him as the big bout approached, she kept it a secret from him. She told him about it after the fight. He admitted later he felt very bad that she had kept this from him, though he understood that she was thinking of him. It was his child, too. Barbara was his wife and the mother of his daughter. They were a family and he wanted to be the man of the family, not an occasional visitor.

She was not to have another child.

He brooded through the preparations for the second Charles fight, which was not like him. As the fight drew near, he bore down and began to concentrate on it; and in the fight he did what had to be done. But after the fight, he went home relieved that it was over. The old excitement seemed to be missing. He was making big money. How much did he need? he wondered. How long could he go on living this unnatural life?

Rocky hangs up his gloves after retiring as world heavyweight champion. Watching is Al Weill, his manager, April, 1956. *Wide World Photo*

11

The Briton and Old Arch

He never would be a stylish fighter, but by 1955, Rocky
Marciano was a frighteningly efficient fighter. He had developed his strength and stamina and punching power to
an awesome degree. Charlie Goldman had taught him well,
and Al Weill had brought him along at a good pace. At
thirty-one, he was a true professional, perhaps as hard to
beat as any man ever had been. He had not been beaten,
despite his stocky build and short arms, despite his lack of
quickness. He fought out of a crouch, bobbing and weaving,
moving in, always moving in, and landing, as often now
with short, devastating punches as with long, wild swings.
He took such punishment as he had to take, and he dealt out
more punishment than most foes could absorb.

Perhaps he was tired of the difficult, demanding life he
led, the constant tension and pressure, the endless training
and traveling, the wear and tear on his body, the absences
from home and the strain he imposed on his family; but in
the ring he remained dedicated to the task at hand, fearless,
furious, concentrating relentlessly on his violent pursuit.

He had begun to reap the rewards of his excellence. Nat

Fleisher's *Ring Magazine,* universally recognized as the bible of boxing and the keeper of records in the sport, had named him "Fighter of the Year" in 1952 and 1954 and had selected his first fight with Walcott in 1952, his second fight with LaStarza in 1953 and his first fight with Charles in 1954 the "Fights of the Year" for those years, and his eighth round against Joe Louis in 1951 and thirteenth round against Walcott in 1952 the "Rounds of the Year" for those years.

The Boxing Writers' Association of New York had in 1952 voted him the Neil Memorial Trophy as the person who had done the most for his sport. Jack Dempsey, Joe Louis, Henry Armstrong, Barney Ross, Ray Robinson and Ezzard Charles had been other winners of the prized award. In his home, Marciano had trophies and plaques and silverware and scrolls which had been given him as honors by persons and groups around the world.

In pursuit of further international recognition and as a way of adding international glamour to his next title defense, Marciano was signed to meet the British heavyweight champion Don Cockell in San Francisco. The bout was set for May, making it eight months from his previous defense and allowing his nose time to heal. The California appearance, set outdoors in Kezar Stadium, was Rocky's second fight out of the Northeast and his first and only fight west of Chicago, although television had made him a well-known figure throughout the country.

There had been few outstanding British heavyweights over the years, and Cockell was so lightly regarded in this country that Marciano was installed as a 7–1 favorite. Perhaps the Marciano camp underestimated Cockell. Perhaps

Marciano did not concentrate on his training as much as usual. In one session, he was caught with a perfect punch by a sparring partner and knocked down, startling him and his handlers. Allie Colombo jumped into the ring and said, "That's all. That's all for today. No one saw it." But many did see it and writers rushed to relay the report. British writers on hand hurried to the nearest cable office to wire the home folks the news that Marciano was no superman, after all.

Weill was upset. As Marciano made a tactful retreat to the showers, Weill was screaming, "That does it. That does it. Get his wife out of camp. Get his kid out. Send 'em home."

San Francisco is a strange sports town, and there was no rush by the citizens to see the fight—a little more than 15,000.

Some say it was the only fight in which Marciano really took his opponent lightly. Cockell was a big, strong fellow who was absolutely unafraid. Marciano was by then acknowledged to be a notoriously slow starter.

Cockell hit him with a hard right hand to the jaw in the first round that caused his knees to buckle for a moment. Rocky grabbed him and held on for a moment, looking over the Briton's shoulder and at his own corner with a startled expression, as if to say, "What the hell is this? Who said this guy was nothing?"

Cockell was something on this night. He was in his prime at 26, had won 61 fights, knocking out 36, including Kid Matthews. Marciano went to work on him, but Cockell gave ground grudgingly. He had been knocked out five times in his career, but for a while he seemed made of stone. For six rounds, he took Marciano's best punches to the head; and while he was gushing blood from the forehead, he stood up and fought back.

In the seventh, Marciano shifted to the body, where the Briton was a bit soft, and the Rock pounded the challenger violently, all but tearing him apart. Late in the eighth round, Rocky switched back to the head, and two long rights dumped Cockell on the ropes. He dangled on them as referee Frank Brown began to count, but at "two" the bell rang.

By the ninth, Cockell seemed exhausted. He was slow and his punches were weak, but he would not quit. Marciano landed a left hook and an overhand right, and Cockell sank slowly to the canvas. As he was sinking, Marciano landed a right hand that spun Cockell into a sitting position.

Slowly, wearily, badly battered, he rose. Marciano tore into him and landed a barrage of lefts and rights as Cockell somehow tried to fight back. A left and a right jolted Cockell's head back and his knees gave out. He crumpled to the canvas again, but slowly, wearily, he rose. The referee now moved in to stop it, hugging the gallant Englishman to his breast and waving one arm to indicate the end of the slaughter.

In Marciano's dressing room, there was relief that plastic surgery on his nose had held up and that Rocky had gotten through the rugged encounter. "He took my best punches," Rocky said with wonder. "No one else took that kind of punishment," Weill added. The battered Cockell wept in his quarters and kept saying over and over again, "He's awkward. He's awkward."

Ted Williams had given Rocky a Boston Red Sox baseball cap. After the fight, the simple, unpretentious champ put in an appearance at an Italian restaurant for a victory feast. His battered face was unshaven. He had on baggy pants. And he was wearing proudly Ted Williams' Red Sox cap.

The next morning, he collected his $130,000 and went home to be with his family. Weill went back to maneuver.

There was one fight Weill could make which would make big money. That was with Archie Moore, the light-heavyweight champion. The only promising heavyweight contender around, Floyd Patterson, the 1952 Olympic champion, was only in his third full year as a pro, had been beaten by Joey Maxim the year before and was not ready for Rocky.

Moore had taken the 175-pound title from Maxim in 1952 and defended it successfully four times. When he knocked out Bobo Olson, the middleweight king, in three rounds in June, he demanded a shot at the heavyweight title. Moore was given to extra weight, and it would be easy for him to build up to Marciano's level.

Moore was thirty-eight years old and had been fighting twenty years, but he was an amazing man. He'd had close to 150 fights and had met the best men in the game for two decades, but had not gotten a chance at a title until late in his career. Once he got it, he won it and held it, seemingly pushed by pride to make the most of his ability after all those years on the road scrambling for a living. Somehow, while older, he was fresher than Louis had been. And he was no dancer like Walcott. He was more like Charles, the only man who had established superiority over him. Moore was a brilliant, shrewd boxer and a tremendous puncher with either hand.

The bout with Marciano was made for September in Yankee Stadium, and while Rocky was installed as a 4–1 favorite, there were those who felt Moore could outsmart and outmaneuver him and had the striking power to hurt him. Articulate, charming and persuasive, old Arch boosted the buildup with tall tales as to how he would destroy the myth of invincibility of the awkward titleholder. As the bout neared, interest in it grew enormously.

Marciano trained hard, but distractedly, at Grossinger's. One morning, he was running with his pal Colombo on a country road. "What do you think about my retiring?" Rocky asked Allie.

Although Allie had discussed it with Rocky and had thought about it, it had always been a "someday" thing, and now he was surprised. "This is the biggest fight you've ever had. You shouldn't be thinking about things like retirement now," he cautioned.

Later, a writer asked Rocky about retirement. Rocky said, "Well, my mother and father and wife would like me to stop fighting. I've been thinking about it."

When Weill heard how Marciano was speaking, he was upset. "What's this you been saying?" he asked the Rock one evening.

"I've been saying this might be my last fight," Marciano said.

"Aw, you'll fight lots more," Weill said.

"I've lost the hunger," Marciano said.

Goldman snorted. "You'd still eat the lock off the re-frigerator door if I took my eye off you a minute."

Rocky said, "I mean I'm not working as hard as I used to. When I start to do that too often I'll get beat, and I don't want to get beat. I don't want Rocky Marciano to beat Rocky Marciano."

"Aw, you're just edgy," Weill said. "You been in camp too long. Sure you'll retire someday. But you're just coming into your own. You got lots of big fights ahead of you. You got lots of money to make. Anyway, put it out of your mind. You got one fight to worry about right now."

And he seemed to end the matter.

During training, Marciano had to fly to New York for a brief bit of busniess. Weill and Colombo went along. They flew back in a small, four-passenger plane. The weather turned bad, and as they danced over the Catskills, the pilot seemed nervous. Weill was on edge, gripping his seat. Allie Colombo was sweating. Rocky calmly read a newspaper as if nothing was happening.

Finally, the pilot spotted Grossinger's barn and put the plane down, though it slid precariously on wet grass for some way before stopping.

Weill jumped up. "That's it! No more plane flights for my million-dollar property!" he yelled.

It was, as it later was to turn out, an ironic moment.

The bout was scheduled for Tuesday, the twentieth, but the threat of Hurricane Ione was so strong that the pro-moters decided to postpone the bout a day, to Wednesday, the twenty-first. Marciano had been through these post-ponements before, including two straight times before the Charles fights, but they never were easy to bear. You train and train and wait and wait and build up to a pitch for the day of the fight and fight night, and suddenly it's off for another day at least and it's a terrible letdown. You have to wait some more and try to get yourself up high again. "When a fight is put off, those twenty-four hours seem like twenty-four years," Marciano once said.

The hurricane altered its course and blew on by, and the fight went on as rescheduled. There was a tremendous crowd on hand, by far the largest of Marciano's career, 61,574 paying customers. Hundreds of thousands jammed theaters or hovered by radios across the land. The live gate just missed landing among the few million-dollar gates in boxing history, but the radio money and the incredible $1,125,000 theater TV money boosted the gross to $2,248,117, making it the second two-million-dollar fight ever, second only to the second Dempsey-Tunney fight, which grossed $2,658,660.

The great stadium seemed twisted by tension as two of the greatest fighters of all time moved at one another. The chunky Negro challenger was like a cobra, striking fast. After conning Marciano cautiously with feints and jabs in the first round, Moore brought everyone watching this fight screaming to their feet in the first minute of the second round. As Marciano hooked a left to Moore's head, Archie stepped inside it smartly and hit him flush on the jaw with a short, strong, sneaky right-hand punch that sapped all the strength from Marciano's powerful body for a split second and dropped him right down to his knees, on the floor, for only the second time in his career. For just a second his eyes seemed vacant, as though his senses had departed. He shook his head, stunned and shaken.

Moore pranced proudly to his corner, as though counting his riches, ready to receive his crown. But, displaying the amazing recuperative powers that he possessed, showing his awesome strength, Marciano snapped to almost instantly and got to his feet by the time referee Harry Kessler had counted four.

Moore, who had bragged he was the greatest "finisher" in boxing history and would never lose a man once he had him hurt, went after Marciano to put him away. But the champion was well schooled and seasoned now, and he moved inside, struggling furiously with his tormentor, giving him no room to measure him. Desperately, Moore tried to wrestle loose, but Marciano kept banging inside. Rocky was bleeding from his nostrils and from a cut above his left eye, but he gradually was regaining his bearings. The bell rang.

Desperately, Weill and Goldman worked on Rocky between rounds. Weill's excitement at such perilous moments had made Rocky frequently wish he would stay out of his corner during fights, but Weill's confidence in his importance to his fighter was such that he shrugged off hints angrily and remained in his tiger's corner.

The bell rang for the third round and the spectators responded with a roar of expectant excitement. Moore had proven he could put Marciano down. He had hurt him, and now the cagey veteran was in a position to make the most of his advantage. And Rocky was angry, which made him careless. He roared after Moore, swinging wildly, as he had earlier in his career. Archie, bobbing and weaving, avoided most of the blows and counterpunched perfectly, drilling short, swift, hurting punches to the champion's head. Two stiff lefts to Marciano's nose drove the champion back. But just before the bell, Marciano landed with a left uppercut that threatened to tear Moore's head from his neck and brought his eyes open wide with wonder.

By the fourth round, Marciano had a grip on himself and was just warming to his task. He drove straight and hard at Moore, punching powerfully. Moore kept jabbing and backing up and slipping punches and looking for an opening to land a big punch, but he could not avoid all of Rocky's crunching blows. In the last minute of the round, Marciano pinned Moore against the ropes and threw every kind of punch imaginable at him, but the experienced and artful Moore hid behind arms and elbows and shoulders and ducked this way and that way in one of the greatest defensive performances of all time. Angrily, punching without letup, Marciano landed a left hand to Moore's head after the bell had rung, and Moore retaliated with a solid right to Marciano's head before the referee intervened.

The fans were in bedlam now. Moore, moving his hands like a magician and his chunky body like a will-o'-the-wisp, outsmarted Marciano through the full three minutes of the fifth round, parrying his bull-like rushes, evading his heavy swings, cracking punches off Rocky's face. But Rocky determinedly kept moving in.

The sixth was a great round, one of the greatest rounds ever. A hard, straight right by Marciano landed high on Moore's head and staggered him, and then a short, chopping, hammerlike right pounded the side of Archie's jaw and sent him staggering to the canvas. But he got up at the count of four and Marciano charged him. Archie covered up and battled back, bobbing away from punches along the ropes and countering strongly, but then a thunderous right hand blasted into Moore's jaw, and he went down for the second time. He was badly hurt now, but not yet finished. Shrugging away pain, he struggled to his feet at the count of eight.

Smiling, he actually advanced on Marciano, dropping his gloves as though to taunt him, seemingly saying to him that he was not afraid of him. Marciano greeted him menacingly, punching to put him away. But for every punch Marciano threw, Moore had one in return. In the last seconds, the two warriors stood toe-to-toe, flailing at each other with frightening fury with the noise of the hysterical crowd raining down on them. At the bell, both seemed to stagger as they returned to their corners. The crowd gave them a standing ovation.

In the seventh, Moore stayed low to protect himself and began to hammer Marciano's midsection. Rocky kept driving punches at him, but he hit a lot of arms. Still, he was wearing Moore down, and Archie slipped to his knees near round's end and arose wearily.

In the eighth, Marciano smashed away relentlessly, but Moore continued to fight back and defended himself skillfully until late in the round, when Rocky drove a hard overhand right to the side of Moore's face, which stunned him. Marciano followed with another right, a left hook and still another right hand, and Moore fell down. The count had reached six and Moore was struggling uncertainly to regain his feet when the bell rang.

Clearly, Moore had little left. Between rounds, Dr. Vincent Nardiello hurried into Archie's corner to look him over, for fear he might be in danger if he was subjected to more punishment. He asked Moore if he'd had enough. Moore said he had not. Moore said he, too, was a champion, and if he went down, he would go down fighting. The doctor shook his head and went away.

In the ninth, Marciano resumed as relentless an attack as the ring had ever seen. Possibly in this fight he threw as many punches as any man ever threw in a single fight. He hammered Moore with lefts and rights and drove him into his own corner. Moore's eyes were badly swollen. Still, he tried, landing a right high on Marciano's face and a right on his jaw. Marciano moved in and drove a lethal left hand under Moore's heart which seemed to stun him, then threw a wide right which crashed against the side of Moore's jaw and contorted his face. Moore started down as Marciano followed with a left hook, which brushed Archie's jaw. Moore descended in his corner, his hair standing on end, his eyes vacant, his mouth open.

He sat there, his legs lying flat on the canvas and spread in front of him, his left hand gripping the middle strand of ropes. Referee Harry Kessler counted over him. As the count reached "eight," Moore tried to pull himself erect, gripping the ropes with both hands, but his legs collapsed under him and he fell back on the ropes as ten was tolled over him.

Marciano, sympathetic rather than ecstatic, went to kneel

by Moore's side, then helped his handlers raise him back onto his feet and lead him back to his corner. The end had come at 1:19 of the round, and the announcer read off the result, which the crowd cheered, and some fans tried to get into the ring to congratulate the champion, but the police pushed them back. Still, it was madness in that ring, Marciano smiling, his hand held aloft by his crew, while Moore stood sadly in his corner, staring at the scene enviously, shifting his gaze to the canvas, his eyes still filmed over and his senses still dazed.

It had been a great fight, which some felt had been the hardest of Marciano's career. Walcott had come as close to knocking him out and closer to outpointing him, yet Moore had seemed to threaten him more. Charles had outboxed him more and had cut him badly, yet had not hurt him as much. Walcott and Charles had carried him farther, but Moore had extended him more and taken more from him. Like Walcott and Charles and LaStarza, too, Moore was never the same again after receiving a terrible beating from Marciano, though old Arch fought on for years.

Rocky picked up his biggest purse, nearly half-a-million dollars for one night's work—$468,374, to be exact—split it with Weill, banked his share after taxes and went home.

Rocky charges into Cassius Clay, in their computer-
ized "super fight," filmed in secrecy in August, 1969.
United Press Photo

12

The End of the Road

Jack Dempsey was in the audience when Marciano finished Moore. He watched the whole fight without saying much to anyone, almost impassively, a man who had been there, himself, one master studying another. But when Marciano sent over those final blows which slugged Moore down for good, Dempsey shook his head with wonder and his mouth opened and he said softly, but with awe, "Murderous puncher."

Asked if he wanted to fight Marciano again, Moore, sagging on a canvas table in his dressing room, looked up at the questioner through his broken face, smiled a little sadly and asked, "Are you crazy?"

He wanted to go on fighting, though, and he feared no man. He seemed to love Marciano for what this man had shown him; and for some time after that, as Moore went on his world tours, he used to send Rocky postcards of one sort or another. One from Spain showed a bullfight scene. Archie had written his own name next to the matador and Rocky's name next to the bull, and he added the message, "Let's do it again." But he never pressed it and Marciano didn't really want it. He didn't really want to fight again. "This is not an easy life," he sighed to one reporter.

He kept thinking about it and thinking about it. Finally, he made a decision. He went to Weill and he said, "Al, I'm going to retire."

Weill may have been startled. It certainly was not a surprise to him, but now it had been presented to him as a very real thing, and he could see a lot of money yet to be made drifting away. Still, he was concerned for his fighter.

"You can retire if you want," he said. "But don't say it, because you can make some money yet."

Rocky said, "No."

Weill asked, "Are you sure? You can take a couple of weeks off and have a little fun and you'll change your mind. While you're still hot we can book an exhibition tour and pick up some quick dough. It's a shame to waste this kind of money."

Marciano wasn't sure. He decided to take the couple of weeks off to think it over. He took his wife to South America for a vacation. He woke up one morning in a hotel lying in bed with Barbara and he sensed that she was feeling bad. He asked her what was wrong. She showed him a small lump on her neck. He asked what it was. She said it was from a gland infection which had arisen four or five times before.

"Why didn't you tell me? Why didn't you see a doctor?" he asked, concernedly.

"I've seen doctors," she said, "but I didn't want to bother you with it. You're always so busy. The doctors say I'll have to go to the hospital to have it taken care of, but I don't want to go without you being around. I'm afraid."

After she fell asleep, he cried. He thought of how she had kept this from him and how she had kept her miscarriage from him earlier.

They went home, where Barbara could go to the hospital to have her condition corrected while Rocky was there.

Meanwhile, a special commission was investigating the boxing situation in California. Here, it was revealed that Jimmy Murray had paid $10,000 off the top of the receipts for the right to co-promote, with the IBC, the Marciano-Cockell bout in San Francisco and that the money had been credited to Al Weill.

Weill denied any impropriety. When Marciano was asked "What about Al Weill and those charges in California that he took $10,000 off your purse?" Rocky said, "I believe Al is an honest guy. We've been together nine years and Al wouldn't do that to me." Later, Marciano insisted, "He never cheated me. He gave me an honest count every time. I wouldn't have been champ without him."

Still, within days, he went to Weill and said, "Al, this is it. I've definitely decided to quit."

Weill shrugged sadly. "OK, if that's what you want," he said.

Jim Norris was there. He asked, "Can we talk about money?"

Marciano said, "No, money's not the question."

He said he had made as much money as he would need; he was tired and he wanted to spend some time with his family. They tried, but could not convince him otherwise. They had no big matches to offer him, anyway.

He was thirty-one years old and had been fighting nine years. He'd been a champion more than three years.

On April 27, 1956, reporters were summoned to a press conference in a private room in the Hotel Shelton in New York where Weill had his office. Marciano sat on a dais with Weill, Goldman and Norris. Rocky wore a blue suit, a white shirt, a white brocaded tie and black shoes. He looked sad.

He announced his retirement. He said it was a hard thing to do. "I was a nobody. In the ring, I became a somebody." He said it was not because he didn't like boxing anymore, "it's being away from the folks, being away from my wife and daughter, never being home.

"Barbara has been after me to quit for some time. I think it would be taking advantage of my family if I tried to fight anymore. When I was single it didn't make any difference. But I'm married now and the baby makes a lot of difference. I want her to have a father and I want her to know him."

There were tears in his eyes. He said, "My mother never really wanted me to fight and never saw me fight, and my decision puts her very much at ease. My father always liked boxing, but he was beginning to feel the strain and he's happy to see me quit."

He paused, then he said, "I'm proud of the record I made. My reputation is clean. And I never was hurt fighting. I have my own home on the outskirts of Brockton. My mother and father and all the kids, who are grown up now, are set up pretty good. I was able to retire my father from the factory in which he worked forty-six years.

"I know people all over the world. I'm buddy-buddy with celebrities. I've even learned what fork to use at fancy dinners." He smiled. "I want to enjoy myself," he said.

"I come from poor people and I know the value of a dollar. I'm pretty well off."

The writers went back to their typewriters and composed fond farewells to the great champ, who had been named "Fighter of the Year" for the third time in 1955; but most speculated that Rocky was too young to retire permanently, and when a new champion emerged impressively, Marciano might well come back to challenge him.

Wherever he went in the next few months, he was pressed about the finality of his retirement. He said, "I've hung up my gloves and I'm not going to get in the ring again except maybe to take a bow. I've got a lot of wonderful memories and I'm not going to spoil them. I'll always remember when Joe Louis came back. Once I retire, I'll never come back."

Someone said, "Nobody'll touch your record, Rock. There's never been another champ who never lost a fight in his whole pro career, and there'll never be another one." And Rocky said, "I'd like to think that's true. I'd like to think that in the rest of my life I'll keep that distinction."

He did.

On the beach in Miami, only three months after his retirement, he started to lift his wife onto his shoulders, clowning around, and he renewed his old back troubles, suffering a ruptured spinal disk which required delicate treatment. If he had any thoughts about coming back, this may have finished them, though he recovered. Still, wherever he went for years afterward, rumors that he was coming out of retirement persisted.

In an elimination tournament to determine his successor, Floyd Patterson outpointed Tommy "Hurricane" Jackson, in June, then knocked out Archie Moore in November to gain the vacated throne. Patterson defended it against mediocre foes four times, then lost it by knockout to Ingemar Johansson in June of 1959. He regained it by knockout of Johansson the following June, repeated against Ingo the following March, defended successfully once more, then was knocked out in one round by Sonny Liston to lose the crown in September of 1962.

Cassius Clay won the championship from Liston by knockout in February of 1964 and held it until convicted on his refusal to accept induction into the Army, which idled him. Jimmy Ellis won an elimination tournament to succeed him, but surrendered the crown to Joe Frazier on a knockout in February of 1970.

Marciano's retirement wrecked the IBC, whose power hung on having the heavyweight champion tied up, and it in time faded from existence, hurt badly by court cases on charges of having conducted a monopoly in violation of antitrust laws. Rocky was sought constantly for a comeback bid for the title, first against Patterson, then against Liston, finally against Clay, although he was almost forty by the time Clay won the crown.

Once Marciano was asked about the sort of money he had been offered for comebacks. He said, "One was almost unbelievable. Financially unbelievable, that is."

"How much?" a writer asked.

"Take a guess," Rocky said.

"One million dollars."

"You're not even warm," Rocky smiled.

"A million and a half?"

"No."

"Two million?" the writer asked, incredulously.

At that, Rocky just grinned.

Later, it was learned he had been offered $2,000,000 to take on Clay in a fight which, with theater television, might have grossed five times that much. And, as it happened, Rocky wanted the money and was curious how he might do against Clay. He isolated himself in a training camp for two weeks in an effort to determine if he could get in shape again. He found he could not. Wistfully, he declined the offer. He would not take even that kind of money if he did not feel he deserved it.

Curiously, while he grossed approximately $1,700,000 in purses in his career and took about half of that as his end, much of the money went to taxes, and through the end of the 1960's more of it was dissipated. He had a tomato-growing outfit with "Jimmy Tomatoes" in Florida, an Italian fast-food franchise, an interior-decorating concern, a nightclub and a bowling alley and other investments, but he was not the big-business type and none of these things prospered. He sold real estate and boats, but it was a struggle.

Rocky was not greedy enough to cash in properly. For instance, book publishers and magazine editors bid for his biography, each with a different writer in mind, and Rocky, who knew most of them, was disturbed lest he offend them by picking one over the others. "Look," Allie Colombo said in the presence of one bidder, "you know Bill here and you trust him. Why don't you just sign up with him and forget it?"

"Allie," Rocky said, "you don't understand. I don't mind knocking a guy out, but I just don't want to hurt anybody's feelings."

Eventually, he sold his story to the *Saturday Evening Post* for a six-part serialization, approving two outstanding writers, Milt Gross of New York and Al Hirshberg of Boston, as the authors. One less writer had his feelings hurt than might have been the case otherwise. And he did other magazine pieces with other writers later.

He hustled for a buck, making banquet speeches and appearing at sportsmen's shows for $1,000 a shot and expenses, cutting some commercials and doing some TV shows, traveling, as it turned out, almost as much as he had when he was champion. His name and prominence never faded and he was honored wherever he went.

Some who were close to him felt he came in time to think he might have acted hastily and perhaps retired too soon, but still he refused to come back. Wistfully, he once observed, "In the old days, anyone who had as many big and tough fights as I had would have made three times as much money."

He was proud of the rough road he had traveled. He said, "Sometimes I don't understand the new breed. So many of them want instant fame like instant coffee."

He bought a spacious house to which he retired with his wife and daughter in Fort Lauderdale, and in 1968 he and Barbara adopted an infant boy, whom they named Rocky

Kevin. Their daughter, Mary Anne, was by then a teen-ager. And the ex-champ was wild about his new son.

Rocky adored the quiet life at home, but had to travel to jobs to keep on top of his expenses. Balding, he bought a toupee which he sometimes wore embarrassedly. He got fat. He lived casually and economically on the road. He often dropped in on friends and stayed at their houses, flopping on a spare bed or sofa. Once, between planes in Atlanta, he slept on the floor of a friend's one-bed hotel room for a couple of hours because he didn't want to bother checking in.

The years drifted by, four years, eight years, twelve years. He seldom went to fights. Once he went to the White House, where he posed for a picture with President Eisenhower and Joe DiMaggio which was reprinted in newspapers across the country. On impulse, he decided to visit his old home-town of Brockton. He didn't even recognize some childhood friends he passed on the street. He heard one mutter to another, "Look at old Rocky. Stuck up ever since he got his picture taken with DiMaggio."

He was included in a "computer tournament," in which information on past heavyweight champions—including John L. Sullivan, Gentleman Jim Corbett, James J. Jeffries, Jack Johnson, Jack Dempsey, Joe Louis and Cassius Clay—was fed into computers and round-by-round bouts were broadcast across the country. It was all utter nonsense, but aroused surprising interest. Rocky could not help but feel some pride when he "knocked out" Jack Dempsey in the final round of the final match to attain ranking as the "all-time king."

Asked how he felt he would have done against Clay,

Rocky said, "I would have liked to have fought him. I always fought the best. Clay could never knock me out. I don't believe anyone could ever have knocked me out. I don't know if he could have outpointed me. No one ever did, but I really don't know if I could have beaten him."

He was asked to take off weight, put on a toupee and stage a mock fight with Clay with all possible endings filmed, which could later be cut to a pattern dictated by the computer and be shown in theaters all over the country. He and Clay both agreed to do it for fees. Marciano did it, but never found out how it came out.

He often reminisced about his fights and frequently went back to the Louis bout, which seemed the turning point and the most dramatic moment in his career. Joe Falls, the fine writer of the *Detroit Free Press* and the *Sporting News,* who admitted he was one who never quite forgave Marciano for knocking out Louis, cornered him in Toronto once and asked him what he remembered about it.

Rocky looked into his coffee cup, and his face grew serious. He started speaking softly. "I remember them holding up my hand, holding it in the air," he said, "and I remember looking down at Joe and feeling this . . . this strange feeling of sorrow come over me. I remember looking out at the crowd and how everyone just sat there in silence. Only the guys from my hometown, Brockton, were making any noise.

"And I remember this girl, this blonde, coming down the aisle and how she was crying and calling me every name she could think of . . . 'You beast . . . you brute . . . you animal.' And she threw this bottle at me and it bounced onto the canvas, and I looked at it, spinning around and around. . . ."

He'd reminisce about his hardest fights, the first one with LaStarza, the one with Layne, the first one with Walcott, the two with Charles, the one with Moore. It all seemed so far away and long ago to others, but to Marciano it was like only yesterday.

But his memories were growing frayed, torn by time. First, Jim Norris died. Then, in November of 1968, Charlie Goldman died at eighty. In January of 1969, a car crash claimed Allie Colombo, who was still young. Marciano mourned.

He went to Chicago to appear at a benefit testimonial to Charles, confined to a wheelchair with lateral sclerosis. It was a wistful time.

On a rainy Sunday night, August 31, 1969, the night before his forty-sixth birthday, he was flying to a speaking engagement in Des Moines in a single-engined, light plane when it crashed in a field in central Iowa, and he was killed.

Less than two months later, on October 20, Al Weill died at the age of seventy-five, virtually broke, in the Crestview Nursing Home in Miami, Florida.

In less than one year, Rocky and Allie, Al and Charlie, the Marciano contingent which captured the heavyweight championship of the world, was wiped out. The old gang was gone.

Rocky had been retired thirteen years when he perished two miles south of Newton, Iowa. The Cessna 172 struck a tree and crashed onto a farm pasture. There were two others aboard, a friend of Marciano's, Frank Farrell, and the pilot, Glen Beltz. They were thrown clear on impact, while Rocky remained trapped in the the cockpit. All were killed.

Later, the National Transportation Safety Board investigated and announced it had found no evidence of mechanical failure or physical impairment with the pilot and that there had been fuel remaining in the tanks. They concluded that the thirty-seven-year-old pilot had crashed because he had flown into stormy weather he was not licensed or experienced enough to handle. He had 230 flying hours, but no instrument rating.

The board report said in part, "The true tragedy of this accident is that it could have been prevented."

The day after his death, Marciano had been due back home, where surprises awaited him. There were presents laid out in the living room to be given him on his birthday. And there was a seventeen-month-old son who had begun to walk since his daddy's departure ten days earlier. Rocky had not been told. His son, whom he adored, was going to show off for him. The child was too young to understand that his daddy was not coming home.

Rocky's mother-in-law, who had been visiting her daughter, stood among the unopened presents, and said, "I don't know what will be done with them. We're not thinking too much about that with what's happening."

She sighed. "All of us find it hard to believe. He didn't know young Rocky could walk. Mary Anne is very upset. Barbara can't talk because she's crying."

The news made front-page headlines in newspapers across

the country and struck many like a thunderbolt. Writers were hard pressed to express the sentiments they felt about this champion they admired so much.

Joe Louis said, "This is the saddest news I've ever heard. When Rocky beat me, I think it hurt him more than it did me. He was always talking about it. After the fight, he sent a message to my dressing room saying how sorry he was the fight turned out the way it did. He just had a good heart. Everything I remember about him is good."

Joe Walcott said, "He was a personal friend of mine. He was pleasant, happy-go-lucky, gentle, kind outside the ring, but he was a lion, a man of courage, in the ring. He was a man all youth looked up to. It's a great loss to everyone."

Ezzard Charles said, "I always liked Rocky. I am very sorry to hear about his death. I just simply can't accept it."

Archie Moore said, "He was a great man and his loss is a tragedy."

Cassius Clay said, "He was so great and so popular and yet he never showed conceit."

When Carmine Vingo awakened the Monday morning after the accident, his wife told him about it. "Maybe you misunderstood," he said hopefully. "Maybe it was somebody else."

But she had the newspaper and she said gently, "No," and she showed him. Vingo was thirty-nine and still partially paralyzed from his bout with Marciano. He didn't want to believe what had happened.

"I don't remember a thing about that bout," he said, "but I remember Rocky. He was a fine man."

Newspapers the world over featured his passing. There

Cadets fold the flag which covered the casket of Rocky during funeral services. Sitting in front row (l-to-r) his brother Louis, his wife Barabara and daughter Mary Ann, September, 1969. *United Press Photo*

were headlines and sad stories and pictures in London and Paris and Rome. In Ripa Teatina, where Rocky had been given a triumphal welcome on a visit in 1964, townspeople milled around the square in tears, consoling relatives of the Marchegianos.

On Tuesday Rocky Marciano's body was flown to Brockton, where thousands were drawn to the casket to pay their last respects at a funeral home. A final tribute came Thursday in a Solemn Requiem Mass at St. Colman's Church, where he had married his sweetheart. Nearly 2,000 persons crowded inside to hear eleven priests participate in the Mass, while another 1,000 stood quietly outside.

Many from the boxing world were there, and some followed the flag-draped coffin on Friday as it was flown on to Fort Lauderdale, where it was displayed in another funeral home. Many came, some in mourning black, some in shorts and sports clothes. An elderly man said, "I met him once and considered him a friend. He didn't know me, but I still considered him a friend."

Joe Frazier was there and Clay and Walcott and Ellis and Joe Louis. The Brown Bomber's eyes were misted with tears. At one point, he slipped quickly away from the crowd to kneel quietly and kiss the top of the casket. "It was like losing someone from my own family," he murmured. "The loss of one of them couldn't have hurt me more."

The funeral was in St. Pius Church. As he approached the casket, the Rev. Vince Adriuska suddenly stopped and said, "God bless you, Rocky."

The long procession began to the burial at Queen of Heaven Cemetery.

On January 20, 1970, nearly fourteen years after his retirement and nearly five months after his death, the seventy rounds Rocky had "boxed" with Cassius Clay the preceding August had been pared to fifteen rounds and were shown in 1,500 theaters across the country.

Entering a theater, Clay was wistful. "He was an old man, and it was only for fun, but my arms hurt for a long time after our 'fight.' Now I believe what people had been telling me about that man's punching power. But as to whether he could have beaten me or whether he does beat me in this, I don't know. A computer decided, but computer's can't fight. It's only make-believe."

It was an odd feeling, watching Marciano fight a make-believe fight which was presented as though it was a "live" show. It was like seeing a ghost. And it was ludicrous, though Marciano did not look too bad. He had trimmed down and his hair-piece stayed in place. He was 45 years old when he staged this last match three weeks before his death, but he went at Clay with some of the old zest. Watching in a Miami Beach theater, his widow, Barbara, said, "It made me shiver."

The computer must have paid some special attention to Marciano's first fight with old Joe Walcott. Clay "knocked down" Marciano in the eighth round and "cut" him over both eyes and had a big lead in points when Marciano began to reach Clay, cornered him on the ropes and "knocked him out" in the thirteenth round.

Clay seemed to enjoy it most of the way. While he was "piling up a lead," he chortled, "You're cooking, champ." Even when he began to "take a beating," he was curiously charitable. "Rocky never hit a man that many times he didn't go down. It takes a good champ to lose like that," he said.

Later he said, "That Marciano was sure a good man, even if maybe he couldn't have whipped me for real." As accomplished, as proud and vain as he was, Clay seemed unwilling to say anything that would spoil the memory of Marciano.

No one ever will know who was the greatest heavyweight boxing champion of all time, but the arguments will rage on forever. Only the record is for certain and it shows that no one Rocky Marciano fought ever beat him in 49 fights, and no other major professional fighter since the turn of the century had completed his career undefeated at the time of Rocky's death.

The old-timers living in the past make cases for some classic names, but the records do not substantiate their claims. Jack Johnson fought 14 draws and was beaten 7 times and knocked out 5 times, for example. Jim Corbett fought only 33 times, had 6 draws and was beaten 5 times, three times knocked out. Jim Jeffries fought only 23 times, drew twice and was knocked out once.

Bob Fitzsimmons really was a middleweight, and he lost 7 times anyway, 6 times by knockouts. Gene Tunney really was a light-heavyweight. He lost only once, to the great Harry Greb, but he also defended the heavyweight title only once. He beat Jack Dempsey twice, but Dempsey was beaten 7 times in all, and also had 8 draws. And he defended his title only 5 times in 7 years.

As the 1970's began, Cassius Clay and Joe Frazier were undefeated throughout their professional careers, but Clay had not yet retired and Frazier did not appear ready to retire. And as boxing seemed to be sliding toward a grave as a major sport in most of the United States, the caliber of their foes had been mediocre. Rocky Marciano was the last heavyweight champion of the last heyday of prizefighting. He fought some great men, though even they were aging then.

On the records, only Joe Louis can be compared to Rocky Marciano as a heavyweight champion. Louis defended his title 24 times, while Marciano defended it only 6 times. But Louis was knocked down many times, while Marciano was knocked down only twice. And Louis was beaten 3 times and knocked out twice while Marciano was never beaten, much less knocked out.

Marciano knocked out 43 of his 49 victims for a KO average of 87 percent, the best in ring history. Louis ranks next best, but far behind with 54 knockouts in 68 bouts for 76 percent. Dempsey knocked out 49 out of 60 for 61 percent. Marciano knocked out more than half his foes within three rounds.

Whether he was or was not the greatest heavyweight champion of all time—and a case can be made for him—he was the most devastating force ever unleashed in a boxing ring.

Outside the ring, he was something else—a gentle, kind man. But it was in the ring that he found fame and reached his destiny, and if he never fully enjoyed his savage sport, he never demeaned it and he never was ashamed of it.

Late in his life, he was asked about two young heavyweights who were not working at their profession with the sort of dedication that had brought Marciano success. Rocky sighed and said, "They don't realize you've got to make boxing a kind of religion. You believe in yourself and you believe in the things you have to do. You never forget them for a minute. Then you get to the top and you think of what you had to go through and you ask yourself, 'Was it worth it?' And it should have been. For me, it cost a lot, but it was worth everything."

ROCCO FRANCIS MARCHEGIANO
(Rocky Marciano)

Born: September 1, 1923, in Brockton, Massachusetts
Married: December 31, 1950 (Barbara Cousens)
Two children: Mary Anne (1953), Rocky (1968, adopted)
Died: August 31, 1969; plane crash in Iowa

ROCKY MARCIANO'S
PRO RING RECORD

Year Bout	Date	Place	Foe	Result	
1947					
1.	March 17	Holyoke, Mass.	Lee Epperson	KO	3
1948					
2.	July 12	Providence, R.I.	Harry Balzerian	KO	1
3.	July 19	" "	John Edwards	KO	1
4.	Aug. 9	" "	Bobby Quinn	KO	3
5.	Aug. 23	" "	Eddie Ross	KO	1
6.	Aug. 30	" "	Jimmy Weeks	KO	1
7.	Sept. 13	" "	Jerry Jackson	KO	1
8.	Sept. 20	" "	Bill Hardeman	KO	1
9.	Sept. 30	Washington, D.C.	Gil Cardione	KO	1
10.	Oct. 4	Providence, R.I.	Bob Jefferson	KO	2
11.	Nov. 29	" "	Pat Connolly	KO	1
12.	Dec. 14	Philadelphia, Pa.	Gilley Ferron	KO	2
1949					
13.	March 21	Providence, R.I.	Johnny Pretzie	KO	5
14.	March 28	" "	Artie Donato	KO	1
15.	April 11	" "	Jimmy Walls	KO	3
16.	May 2	" "	Jimmy Evans	KO	3
17.	May 23	" "	Don Mogard	W	10

187

18.	July 18	" "	Harry Haft	KO	3
19.	Aug. 16	New Bedford, Mass.	Pete Louthis	KO	3
20.	Sept. 26	Providence, R.I.	Tom DiGiorgio	KO	4
21.	Oct. 10	" "	Ted Lowry	W	10
22.	Nov. 7	" "	Joe Domonic	KO	2
23.	Dec. 2	New York City	Pat Richards	KO	2
24.	Dec. 19	Providence, R.I.	Phil Muscato	KO	5
25.	Dec. 30	New York City	Camine Vingo	KO	6

1950

26.	March 24	New York City	Roland LaStarza	W	10
27.	June 5	Providence, R.I.	Eldridge Eatman	KO	3
28.	July 10	Boston, Mass.	Gino Buonvino	KO	10
29.	Sept. 18	Providence, R.I.	Johnny Shkor	KO	6
30.	Nov. 13	" "	Ted Lowry	W	10
31.	Dec. 18	" "	Bill Wilson	KO	1

1951

32.	Jan. 29	" "	Keene Simmons	KO	8
33.	March 20	Hartford, Conn.	Hal Mitchell	KO	2
34.	March 26	Providence, R.I.	Art Henri	KO	9
35.	April 30	" "	Red Applegate	W	10
36.	July 12	New York City	Rex Layne	KO	6
37.	Aug. 27	Boston, Mass.	Fred Beshore	KO	4
38.	Oct. 26	New York City	Joe Louis	KO	8

1952

39.	Feb. 13	Philadelphia, Pa.	Lee Savold	KO	6
40.	April 21	Providence, R.I.	Gino Buonvino	KO	2
41.	May 12	" "	Bernie Reynolds	KO	3
42.	July 28	New York City	Harry Matthews	KO	2
43.	Sept. 23	Philadelphia, Pa.	Joe Walcott	KO	13*

1953

44.	May 15	Chicago, Ill.	Joe Walcott	KO	1*
45.	Sept. 24	New York City	Roland LaStarza	KO	11*

1954

46.	June 17	New York City	Ezzard Charles	W	15*
47.	Sept. 17	New York City	Ezzard Charles	KO	8*

1955

48.	May 16	San Francisco, Cal.	Don Cockell	KO	9*
49.	Sept. 21	New York City	Archie Moore	KO	9*

(Announced retirement, 1956)

*—Heavyweight title bout.

SUMMARIES

All Bouts		Title Bouts
Number	49	6
Won KO	43	5
Won decision	6	1
Lost	0	0
Draws	0	0

Professional career from March 17, 1947, to September 21, 1955—7½ years. Fought 28 times in Providence, R.I., 34 times in New England area. Fought 6 times in New York City, only two times out of East. Scored 11 KO's in first round, 7 in second round, 8 in third round. Held title from September 23, 1952, to September 21, 1955—3 years. Defended title 6 times. Retired as one of only four men who were undefeated during their professional careers. Others, all pre-1900: Jack McAuliffe, 53 bouts, 1884–1897; Larry Foley, 22 bouts, 1866–1888; and Jim Barry, 70 bouts, 1891–1899. Also undefeated as of September, 1970: Cassius Clay, 29 bouts, and Joe Frazier, 25 bouts.

DETAILS OF MARCIANO'S KEY BOUTS

Nontitle

Date	Foe	Location	Attendance	Receipts
Dec. 30, 1949	Carmine Vingo	MSG, N.Y.	9,277	$ 26,325
March 24, 1950	Roland LaStarza	MSG, N.Y.	13,658	53,723
July 12, 1951	Rex Layne	MSG, N.Y.	12,565	73,195
Aug. 27, 1951	Freddie Beshore	BG, Boston	9,523	26,953
Oct. 26, 1951	Joe Louis	MSG, N.Y.	17,241	152,845
Feb. 13, 1952	Lee Savold	PCH, Phila.	9,243	61,386
July 28, 1952	Harry Matthews	YS, N.Y.	31,188	215,708

Title

Date	Foe	Location	Attendance	Receipts
Sept. 23, 1952	Joe Walcott	PCS, Phila.	40,379	504,645
May 15, 1953	Joe Walcott	CS, Chicago	16,034	331,795
Sept. 24, 1953	Roland LaStarza	PG, N.Y.	44,562	435,817
June 17, 1954	Ezzard Charles	YS, N.Y.	47,505	543,092
Sept. 17, 1954	Ezzard Charles	YS, N.Y.	34,330	352,654
May 16, 1955	Don Cockell	KS, S.Fran.	15,235	196,720
Sept. 21, 1955	Archie Moore	YS, N.Y.	61,574	948,117
Title Totals	7 bouts		259,639	$3,312,840

MARCIANO TITLE GATE-TV PURSES

	Gate	TV
1. Walcott	$ 69,085	$ 25,000
2. Walcott	76,038	90,000
3. LaStarza	141,624	53,125
4. Charles	200,586	47,452
5. Charles	120,608	54,000
6. Cockell	64,496	50,000
7. Moore	328,374	140,000
Total.........................		$1,460,338

Note

MSG—Madison Square Garden, N.Y.   CS—Chicago Stadium
BG—Boston Garden, Boston   PG—Polo Grounds, N.Y.
PCH—Philadelphia Convention Hall   YS—Yankee Stadium, N.Y.
KS—Kezar Stadium, San Francisco

HEAVYWEIGHT CHAMPIONSHIP HISTORY

Champion	Age Won Title	Reign	No. Defenses	Duration	Pro Record W–L–D*	KO's
1. John L. Sullivan	23	2/82–9/92	3	10½ yrs.	31– 1–43	16
2. James J. Corbett	26	9/92–3/97	2	4½ yrs.	20– 5– 8	9
3. Bob Fitzsimmons	35	3/97–6/99	1	2 yrs.	28– 7– 5	23
4. James J. Jeffries (X)	24	6/99–7/04	7	5 yrs.	20– 1– 2	16
5. Marvin Hart (#)	29	7/05–2/06	1	7 mos.	29– 8–12	20
6. Tommy Burns	24	2/06–12/08	12	2½ yrs.	46– 5– 9	36
7. Jack Johnson	30	12/08–4/15	7	6½ yrs.	83– 7–28	42
8. Jess Willard	33	4/15–7/19	2	4 yrs.	24– 6– 5	20
9. Jack Dempsey	24	7/19–9/26	6	7 yrs.	60– 7–14	49
10. Gene Tunney (X)	28	9/26–7/28	2	1½ yrs.	56– 1–19	41
11. Max Schmeling (#)	27	6/30–6/32	2	2 yrs.	56–10– 5	39
12. Jack Sharkey	28	6/32–6/33	1	1 yr.	38–13– 4	15
13. Primo Carnera	27	6/33–6/34	2	1 yr.	86–13– 1	66
14. Max Baer	25	6/34–6/35	1	1 yr.	65–13– 1	50
15. James J. Braddock	30	6/35–6/37	1	2 yrs.	51–22–12	26
16. Joe Louis (X)	23	6/37–3/49	24	11½ yrs.	68– 3– 0	54
17. Ezzard Charles (#)	29	6/49–7/51	9	2 yrs.	96–25– 1	58
18. Joe Walcott	37	7/51–9/52	1	1 yr.	49–17– 1	30
19. Rocky Marciano (X)	29	9/52–4/56	6	3½ yrs.	49– 0– 0	43
20. Floyd Patterson (#)	21	6/56–6/59	5	3 yrs.	—	—
21. Ingemar Johansson	26	6/59–6/60	1	1 yr.	25– 2– 0	17
— Floyd Patterson	25	6/60–9/62	3	2 yrs.	46– 7– 1	35
22. Charles (Sonny) Liston	28	9/62–2/64	3	1½ yrs.	51– 4– 0	39 (I)
23. Cassius Clay (Z)	22	2/64–2/68	6	4 yrs.	29– 0– 0	23 (I)
24. Jimmy Ellis (#)	28	2/68–2/70	2	2 yrs.	27– 6– 0	12 (I)
25. Joe Frazier	26	2/70–	0	—	25– 0– 0	22 (I)

Notes

*–Draw totals also include "no-decision" and "no-contest" rulings prevalent in early years.

(X)–Retired while still champion.

(#)–Won general recognition as champion in elimination bout.

(Z)–Deprived of title by inactivity.

(I)–Record incomplete. Still active or not officially retired as of September, 1970.

MEASUREMENTS OF SOME CHAMPIONS

	Hgt.	Wgt.	Reach	Neck	Chest	Waist
Marciano	5-10½	184	68	16¾	39	32
Fitzsimmons	5-11¾	172	71¾	15	41	32
Jeffries	6-2½	225	76½	18¼	43	35
Johnson	6-1¼	222	74	17½	37½	36
Willard	6-6¼	252	83	17½	46	35½
Dempsey	6-1	191	77	16½	42	33
Tunney	6-½	192	77	17	42	34½
Louis	6-1½	218	76	17	42	36½
Charles	6-0	184½	74	16½	39	33
Walcott	6-0	195	74	17	40	35
Patterson	6-0	190	71	17	40	32½
Liston	6-1	212	84	17½	44	33
Clay	6-2½	210	82	17	42	34
Frazier	5-11½	205	73½	17½	42	34